A Letter to

POPE
FRANCIS

Musings On What Ails The Catholic Church

A Letter to

POPE FRANCIS

Musings On What Ails The Catholic Church

ROMÉO GAUVREAU, B.A.,

ARPress
ILLUMINATING IDEAS.
EMPOWERING VOICES

ARPress
45 Dan Road Suite 5
Canton, MA 02021

Hotline: 1(888) 821-0229
Fax: 1(508) 545-7580

Ordering Information:
Quantity sales. Special discounts are available on quantity purchases by corporations,associations, and others. For details, contact the publisher at the address above.

Printed in the United States of America.

ISBN-13:   Softcover   979-8-89356-032-9
              eBook   979-8-89356-033-6

Library of Congress Control Number: 2024902953

TABLE OF CONTENTS

Special Thanks

First, I dedicate this book to my mother, Mélanie Caron Gauvreau, whose insight and courage,

In the face of a life of subjugation, has inspired me with this book writing.

To my elementary school teacher, Miss Estelle Landry who has taught me how to read and write, to my students and to all the students at the school of life.

To my children, François, Bernard and Annie, to Judy`s children, Grant and Craig.

To my granddaughter, Charlotte Nicole, and to this woman who has witnessed my descent in hell too many times, and has received me with open arms on my way back, my wife Judy.

LETTER TO POPE FRANCIS

Dear Pope Francis,

Please, forgive me if I sound a bit inexperienced. It's not every day I write letters to popes! I usually am too busy… I guess I better have a good reason to disturb a man as busy and as important as you are…

Well, I believe I do. I saw your arrival on the Catholic Church scene as a breath of fresh air. I find it interesting from the point of view of an agnostic. I was born a Catholic, but when I was around 25, I gave up my membership card to your club!

Now, if you don't mind, from here on, I'll call you Mario Jorge, my brother, with great respect and affection. I don't like the "Hollywoodian" connotation of King or Pope. It sounds too condescending and haughty for me. I'll explain later on and I believe you'll understand where I'm coming from.

So here's the reason I'm addressing you in my book. From what I read and heard about you in the news and other, you don't belong there. I mean, look at all these mostly conceited, old and "crystallized in their ways" members of the Holy See who are scared senseless of your next move.

No, you don't belong in the **"old"** Catholic Church. You represent a big threat to most of them, since they have been involved in all kinds of dirty work of which the most publicized recently is the sexual abuse by priests, and its covering up by bishops, cardinals and …popes!

The covering up of sexual abuses by priests instead of turning them in to the legal authorities and, in doing so, stop them dead in their tracks, is a very serious crime and we know your strict position on that delicate subject. And while they were at it, they should have turned themselves in for their complicity after the fact.

They are shaking in their boots and for good reasons. I believe you're not the type to take these matters lightly. You have demonstrated that you're not a conformist ...like most of your colleagues are. You don't have the delusion of grandeur, you're not thirsty for power and you have a big heart; we can see it beat through your cassock...

Here's what I would like you to do for the children of the world, for their mothers, for all the women in the world and for humanity in general. As it would be too long to address these matters in a letter format, I chose to write a book dedicated to them —and to you, Brother.

My book will sound accusatory and harsh at times, and I'm aware of it. We have been silent for 2,000 years. Heads have fallen right and left by the thousands (...inquisition). Then some of us have dared try to talk to the Church politely, with the low voice of a slave prostrate in front of his tyrannical master, - the almighty catholic church- .... for far too many centuries ...and look where it has left us!

Try to read my book with fresh eyes, from my point of view, ... from the point of view of the children of the world, from the point of view of the women of the world and of the whole humanity who has the right to its spiritual freedom from a toxic brainwashing by an archaic religion and the right and the access to a loving God, not a judging and condemning God ...for a change!!!

You're a very good man, please do not let these people down; they're counting on you. We know of nobody else that could clean up the mess left by your predecessors —as only you can.

I'm leaving you with a quote: Einstein was not talking about you, I'm sure. You're not the type!

"The world will not be lost by those who do evil but by those who watch them without doing anything."

Albert Einstein

From one of your admirers with brotherly Love,

Roméo

PREFACE

This book contains situations and images that are not appropriate for the whole family! It is recommended for age 18 and over, but not for those who do not have an open mind or are easily offended. It contains very religious, but not very catholic views... I must say that there will be scenes of nudity ...but only of my soul laid bare!

The road on which we choose to follow the herd, regardless of its direction, is not a safe road. In doing so, I think we must deny ourselves; we betray who we really are. We become incidental while we should become instrumental.

It doesn't say on the cover, but this is an essay ...only an essay. My name is not Pope Benedict XVI, I am not infallible. I guess I'm as much infallible as he is, which isn't saying much. But what I'm writing, I believe and I am ready to treat your criticisms with attention and respect.

I do not write to provoke. The title of this book is nothing but my reflections regarding the precarious situation where the Catholic Church finds itself in 2023. Either you, Pope Francis, will do a big cleanup at the Vatican, or that religion might be forced to close its doors.

I grew up in the catholic religion or, rather, in the cult some honor with the title of religion. A marginal benefit of my religion is that, without it, —or another misogynistic religion like it— I wouldn't be here writing at this very moment...

You see, I am the *fifteenth* child in my family. In some ways, I am the by-product of a religion that dictated the reproduction of children to people who knew how to make them and maybe how to stop … but were not allowed to!!! I will definitely return to this subject in this exchange with you.

INTRODUCTION

"Great news, rarely heard news! The pope has resigned!" What's up with that? Popes do not resign; they die pope! This last one, Benedict XVI, has resigned during his lifetime and *of his own will.* During his lifetime, yes! Of his own will? ...That remains to be seen!

I intend to demonstrate, in the pages that follow, that, following the judicial proceedings against the Vatican in recent years, the Catholic Church is facing a very serious problem. The pot is boiling and the lid of the pressure cooker threatens to blow up at any moment. The church no longer has the option of playing hide and seek with the law.

We will look together at all the issues which, I think, are threatening the survival of the Church and I'll suggest possible solutions. I believe that we are witnessing the turning point of a religious empire that threatens to collapse like the Roman Empire did in 476 A.D. Its foundations are shaking and its structure is threatening to collapse. We can continue to bury our heads in the sand; it will not change one iota to the situation. The Catholic Church is facing its most serious crisis since the Inquisition. In the twelfth century, the Catholic religion committed unspeakable crimes without the rest of the Catholics in the world knowing about it right away. In 2023, things are different.

Having to introduce a topic as well known as "religion" seems somewhat superfluous, to say the least. But maybe, just maybe, we do not all have the same concept as to what we vaguely call: religion. If we look at the definition of religion in Wikipedia, we find that "a religion is an organized set of beliefs, cultural systems, and worldviews that connect humanity to an order of existence."

There are as many definitions as there are religions ...and maybe religious people. But the fact remains; it boils down to beliefs, cultural views, opinions and many other factors. There is nothing that causes a strong reaction like to talk about the Catholic religion in the presence of members of that religion. They should not feel threatened; after all ...they have the truth, the whole truth, and nothing but the truth. Besides, God is on their side! Why are they so quick to go for the jugular? I think there are several reasons for their reaction and we will have the opportunity to speak at length about it in the following chapters. To all of you, dear readers, who have accepted my invitation to share some thoughts and ideas through the pages that follow, I say a warm thank you! Just as one is not a stand-up comedian without an audience in need of laughters, one is not a writer without the readers. I need you to receive me, I need to confide in you and share all those thoughts that weigh me down..

I chose to add a few poems to my essay, which I hope, will add softness to the spirit and the atmosphere of the exchange. Here is the first poem I composed a few years ago, and that I reproduce here for you. I hope you'll enjoy it.

Please fasten your seat belts; there could be some turbulence on this trip… I hope you'll have as much fun reading this book as I had writing it. Enjoy! ...and good reflection.

SAY BROTHER, SAY SISTER

Will you help me

When we meet on the often dusty roads of life?

Please will you help me through the maze

That those dusty roads often form?

Through the endless paths with the ill illuminated cul-de-sacs,

Where I roam too often aimlessly,

Between those high walls offering slits of skies but no exits?

Those high walls who, too often, talk of hopelessness, fear and despair?

Say brother, say sister

Will you help me shift my sight from those walls of resistance

Towards those slits of sky full of light and promises?

Will you show me how to decorate those walls

With arrangement of pebbles of color,

Using the mud from the path as cement to form many flowers of many petals?

Say brother, say sister

Will you help me draw on these walls,

Straighter paths with happy destinations?

And thus help me enjoy the journey?

Remind me that happiness is not a destination,

But a way of travelling?

A journey made of moments pregnant of anticipation and discovery?

Say brother, say sister

Will you help me shift my sight from your tired body

To those slits in your face, to the smile on your lips,

To the twinkle in your eyes?

These portals of your heart, these doors to your soul,

Inviting me to a sweet rocking?

In that refuge full of hospitality,

Help me find myself, help me find my way?

Let me see your uniqueness,

your Source energy, your divine ancestry.

Let me see the light reflecting from every fiber of your spiritual being.

Let me reflect in these mirrors of your soul

that are your mysterious eyes.

And doing so,

Let me realize how much we're alike,

in beauty, in grandeur,

in heart hospitality.

Say brother, say sister

Will you help me see all that in you, in me, in all that is?

If you do that for you, for me, for others,

You will be the best teacher,

of light, of life, of possibilities,

of happiness eternal;

of Love.

Say brothers, say sisters

I Love you, all of You.

Roméo Gauvreau, poem composed the morning of an event and delivered at a poetry slam in Bali, Indonesia, May 2006

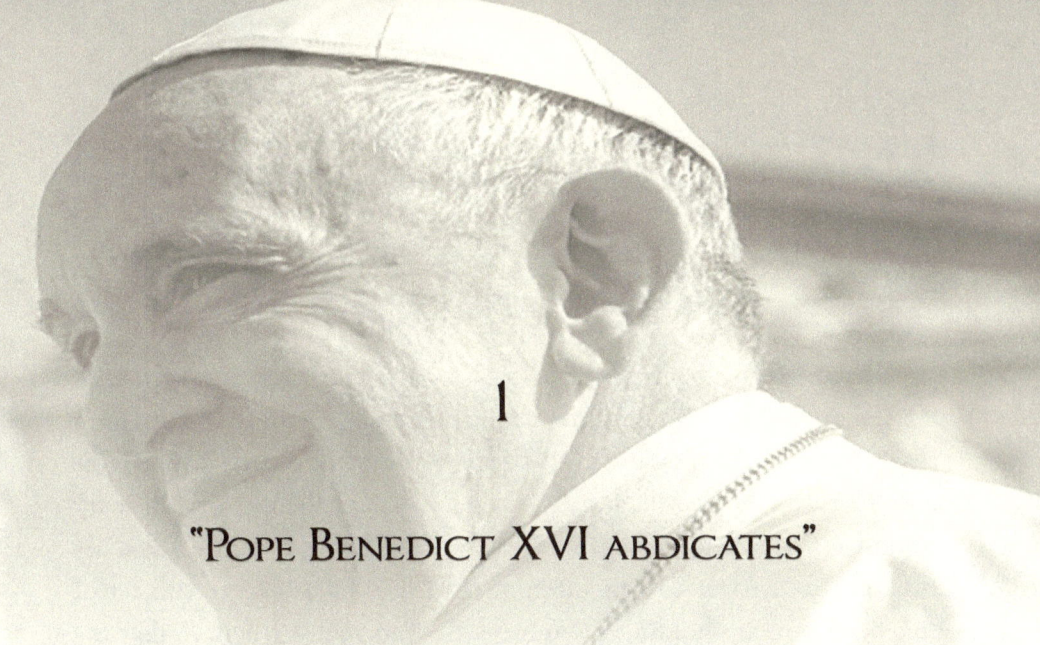

1

"POPE BENEDICT XVI ABDICATES"

"Historic day Thursday in the Vatican for the first time in centuries, a pope, namely Benedict XVI, will leave in his lifetime and of his own desire the throne of St. Peter."

Agency France-Press, Vatican City

February 27, 2013, "Pope Benedict XVI abdicates!" The news went around the world like wildfire. With the force of a tsunami, the news of that event surprised and amazed the world of Christianity. The last time a pope abdicated was around 600 years ago.

Why did he resign? According to the press release, it's for health reasons. There is no doubt that the function of a pope is very time consuming and requires a lot of energy, especially at the advanced age of 85. In recent years, there has been an increasing pressure on the Vatican from various organizations and some members of the Church to act promptly and address the avalanche of sexual abuse scandals by pedophile priests.

"The United Nations anti-torture watchdog has ordered the Vatican to hand over files containing details of clerical sexual abuse

allegations to police forces around the world amid concerns over the use of "diplomatic immunity" to hamper investigations. "

By John Bingham, Religious Affairs Editor

The situation is serious; the Vatican can't play hide and seek with the law anymore. Serious crimes committed in large numbers have been swept under the carpet and the Vatican has to put its cards on the table ...all its cards! How will the Vatican meet this challenge, or will it try to dodge the bullet once again? Dear readers and you, Mario Jorge my brother, the answer to this question and more will be the subject of this book you are holding in your hands. Personally, I believe that the ex-pope has resigned because he was –and still is– facing charges for being involved in hiding pedophile priests from the law when he was a cardinal in Germany.

As a Pope, he has ordered the bishops all over the world to cover up the crimes of the pedophile priests and pay parents to buy their silence and the silence of the victims. And he backed his demand with the explicit threat of excommunication if they didn't comply; excommunication of the bishop, of the victim and of the parents if they break the secrecy pact! Does that sound like Godly love to you, Mario Jorge my brother? Are we talking about a Church, here, or about an organized crime family? I find it flabbergasting, to say the least!!!

In the world at large, the real world, hiding a criminal from the law is as serious as the crime committed by the person one is trying to protect. It's called accessory after the fact. In theory, the ex-pope should go to jail. In practice, that's another question. The prison is good for "nobodies" like us, but not for the high ranked religious or political people... THEY have connections in high places!!! (Corporations? Heaven?)

But Mario Jorge my brother, we have a new player in the field! It has replaced number 16. He has the number 1 on his jersey. Everybody believes and hopes that he is number 1... We know him under the name of Francis ...or Pope Francis. Oh! Let's watch!

2

JORGE MARIO BERGOGLIO, YOU'RE OUR MAN!

"I ask you to be revolutionaries. Have the courage to go against the current. And also have the courage to be happy. "

Pope Francis, July 28 speech to the volunteers of WYD, Rio de Janeiro.

First I must say that without knowing you, Mario Jorge, my brother, other than by the news on TV, I find you very charismatic. You are not crystallized in the old ways and conservative like some of your colleagues… You don't seem to care particularly for "the protocol due to your high rank" –and that, I like from you. I also find you very brave to accept this function …in the circumstances. I think you really want to rectify the criminal conduct of the Church in its dealing with children sexual abuses, which, until now, have been covered up by the Vatican, at least for the last 60 years. There are thousands of priests, bishops, and cardinals, on top of your predecessor himself, who are guilty of cover up.

I believe you would also consider admitting women to the rank of priest. The misogynist attitude of the Catholic Church is well known and appears to be a shameful anachronism that must end without delay.

Finally, the marriage of priests must not only be accepted, but strongly encouraged –if not required. That would be a first step towards the diminution –if not the cessation–of the children sexual abuse by priests.

If you make one or more of these changes, you will probably face a very serious open …and secret opposition from the Holy See. Your life could be …and probably, would be in danger!!!.

One thing that should help and comfort you, Mario Jorge, my brother, is the fact that you have a large part of the population of the world supporting you. The changes you will bring about have been greatly sought out and expected for quite some time.

Personally, I believe that your mission will not be easy. Not because of negative reactions on the part of the members of the Catholic Church at large, but on the part of the Holy See who is not ready to get out of the deep ruts it has settled down in. All were the product of an archaic religion, which, by a strict indoctrination, has conditioned most of them to live in delusion for most of their adult lives.

The challenge is of a "David and Goliath" magnitude, I'm sure, but you have the determination of a man on a mission, a mission that holds you at heart. You can be assured, Mario Jorge, my brother, that we have our shoulder to the wheel and are cheering for you.

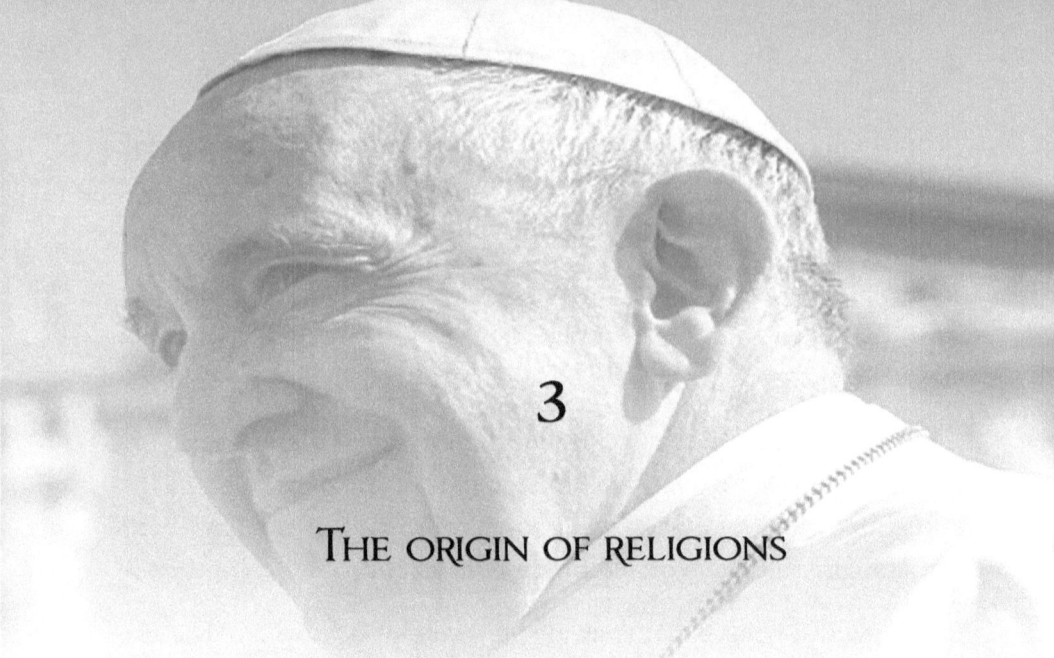

3

THE ORIGIN OF RELIGIONS

"Jesus is ideal and wonderful, but you Christians, you are not like Him."

Mahatma Gandhi

I guess I could stop here and you would have a pretty good idea of what I'm talking about... But there's a lot more I want to say. There's a lot more I need to say! But let's see if we can find the origin of religions.

First, I have to admit that I don't know when religions started. Nobody knows. We know nothing on this Good Earth. We guess, we figure, we imagine, we pretend that we know, etc. Except if one is Catholic. Oh! Those people know everything! They knew thousands of years ago "that the earth is flat!!!" that God created Adam and Eve 6,000 years ago and they know where! They even know some details that some of the non-religious -or stupid peoples like us- don't know... Like the fashion trend of the era: grapevine leaves were apparently the Calvin Klein of the Garden of Eden... Who could have guessed?

Religion, undoubtedly, proves to be the greatest common denominator of human beings. Very few people do not or have not belonged to a religion, which, most of the time, was transmitted and imposed on them by their parents or their ambiant culture.

The small group who started the Catholic religion was probably well-meaning and wanted to help people. A phenomenal person conceived in strange circumstances, perhaps, was apparently an out of the ordinary Messiah! If we believe the story, he could cure any illness and even bring the deceased back to life!

Like you, Mario Jorge, my brother, he was preaching a nonviolent approach to life and even recommended people to love their enemies… His teachings were very revolutionary. Consequently, he had problems with the establishment; he was a nonconformist! But we must remember that Jesus did not found any religion!

Until very recently, in the entire world, we were born into a certain religion and would die in that religion. That religion was dictating to us what to think and what to do and what not to think and what not to do. We were being programmed like robots and we would become pawns in the hands of the Church…and of the government.

After following the gang for as long as we could remember, having been led to believe by force that they had the truth and that the only salutary and true path was theirs, it's not easy to decide and abandon the gang's trail to find your own path, *the only true path!* But at some point in life, whoever we are, we will be faced with the decision to continue –or not–to follow the path most taken, in which you might or might not feel comfortable. And if you don't feel comfortable on that path and don't leave it, you deny and betray who you know and feel in your guts that you really are. The better choice is to trust yourself, take a risk, and give yourself the respect you deserve. There's nobody better than you in the world to be at the helm of your life.

Seriously, I think that religions started when the first earthlings saw something they couldn't explain and fear traumatized them. Like the thunder, forest fires started by the thunder, tornadoes, earthquakes and any phenomenon they couldn't explain. Also a possibility is the fact that tribe leaders found out pretty fast that they could manipulate people trembling with fear by manipulating their beliefs. They could have convinced these people that if they would offer valuable things to the gods, these would protect them …or other fallacies of that nature. And, those leaders, those shamans, those religious leaders (not to say priests…) would end up with the loot. One just has to look at the Vatican's and the Catholic Church's real estate for an example of what I'm talking about…

"When the missionaries came to Africa they had the Bible and we had the land. They said, "Let us pray." We closed our eyes. When we opened them we had the Bible and they had the land."

Desmond Tutu

To me, religion, in lots of cases, is nothing more than the conditioning of the psyche of people with beliefs that feed on their fears and give them a false sense of hope and security, face to the unknown of life and of the afterlife. Religious people first are programmed by a religion's beliefs imposed on them by parents and ''reinforced'' by the church when they're young and they keep it as adults, because they have been strongly brainwashed and don't have the ability …or the right to think for themselves. And when they become adults, the more insecure and conditioned they are, the more they cling *to that mumbo jumbo placebo*. In other words, the more gullible they are, the more chances they have of remaining religious… I'm sure that you don't see religion the way I do, but believe me, I'm not insensitive to your feelings. At least, Mario Jorge, my brother, *could we agree to disagree?*

8

If I had to pinpoint what motivates people to remain in the imposed religion, I would have to say: people's insecurity, intellectual laziness and intellectual dishonesty they learn in school…*and in church*. It is easier to fall asleep and forget than to be alert and continue to question life and our being, to be able to face life without guarantees …or soothing crutches, before daring to take another step …and to assume our human destiny!

"I do not feel obliged to believe that the same God who has endowed us with sense, reason, and intellect has intended us to forgo their use."

Galileo Galilei

But, if you allow me to think a bit more outside the box, I would say something that not everybody is ready to swallow. There are very plausible reasons to believe that around or before Jesus birth some people might have encounter alien visitors in their "charriots of the gods." These aliens, more advanced that we are now, wouldn't even have had to try to make these primitive people believe they were gods. Just their body extensions(flying machine with wings) descending from heaven, was already a sign of power far above their capacity of comprehension and they could only identify them as gods.

These ETs could do everything our technology can do today and a lot more, and in all fields of science and technology, medicine, engineering, chemistry, electronic etc. …*and even the manipulation and exploitation of people, probably?*

Haven't we seen an example of manipulation of less advanced people, when, after the discovery of America, some Aborigines, both in Canada and the USA, got screwed up in their dealings with the white people? From peltries to some young girls, to their land, everything could be settled with mirrors, "trinkets and wiskey", and eventually with new gods; we were the ETs for them.

Around 1950, in a remote place of Africa, a small airplane crashed. It didn't take long for some peoples to build a kind of repository on which they hoist the small airplane and started worshiping it' like God's vehicle. For all they knew, it was a messenger of God or God himself for these poor ignorant and fearful people.

Well, Mario Jorge, my brother, I hate to tell you that, in 2023, over 80% of us humans are these poor ignorant and fearful people...

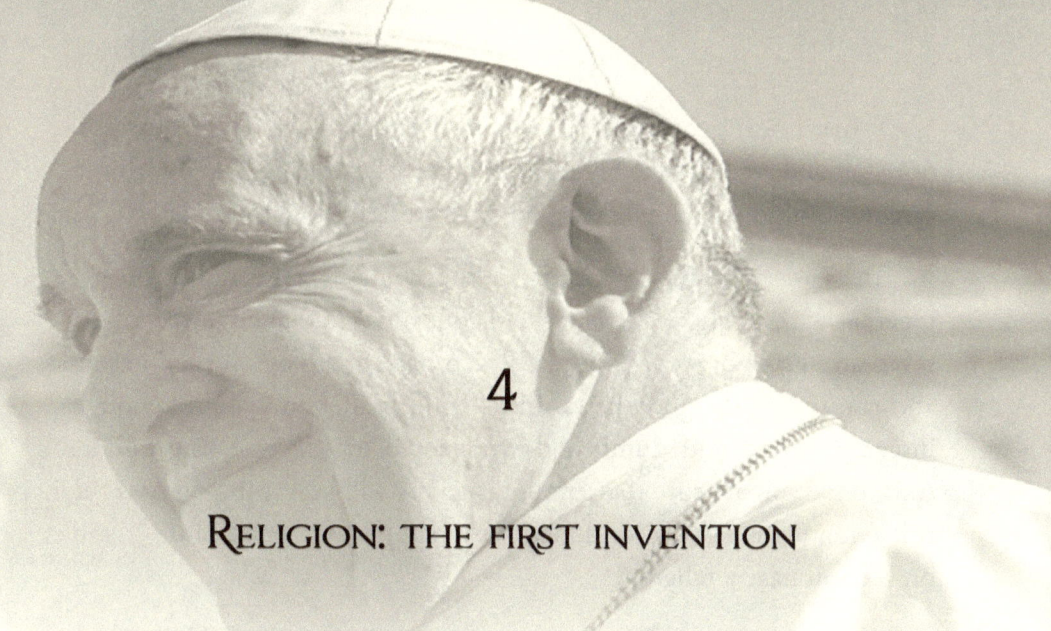

4

Religion: the first invention

All national

"Christian or Turkish, appear to me no other than human inventions, set up to terrify and enslave mankind, and monopolize power and profit."

Thomas Paine

That religion is a great invention shouldn't surprise anybody. Voltaire said that *"if God didn't exist it would be necessary to invent Him."* I must clarify my position here. I am definitely not a religious person, Mario Jorge, my brother, but at the same time, I am not an atheist. I don't believe in the god of Christian religions, but I believe in the possibility of a certain kind of god. I'm fussy about the god I want, though... If there is no other god than the one of the Catholic Church, I'll have to pass... I don't want a judging god, a punishing god, a mean god and one who came unprepared and then had to interfere (incarnate) in human affairs to repair man's mistakes ...i.e. His mistakes!

When I hear people pray to win the lotto, pray for rain, or for sun, or to get laid etc., I shake my head in disbelief and can't help but think: can an omnipotent, intelligent god have created those nimrods?

The easiest business to start in the world is a religion. You get together with a couple of friends and concoct a story about a way to get saved and go to heaven. You start a web page or a blog on the internet and you spread the good news. In no time at all, you will find enough insecure, scared and dumbed down people to start meeting online. And, once you are sure that enough suckers will go for it, you pass the collection plate, i.e. ask for donations to support the good cause ...and bravo! You have a religion!

You are now the CEO of a very prosperous enterprise fed by suckers and gullible nimrods who think they're buying a condo in heaven with a view ...on thin air. That business is tax free and is protected by the right of association. It's the way many religions have started online or otherwise. Not that it was that crapulous in most cases, but lots of them have been started by fanatics who loved power and prestige ... and money. Some called them enlightened or gurus or preachers. I have a limited vocabulary; I call them sociopaths or in a vulgar form: con artists.

Mario Jorge, my brother, I believe there should be very strict laws prohibiting the invention and proliferation of religions. It could be called: the law to protect gullible people from unscrupulous enlightened gurus. But governments benefit from the dumbing down of people by religions and by the school. These religions keep people indoctrinated, or in modern language, brainwashed or, better still: dumbed down... They become subservient and obedient followers. They have been taught to obey orders without questioning them! That's the type of citizens that keep the *"status quo"* alive and well in our societies.

In all justice, I must clarify something I just said. When I say that religion dumbs people down , I must add that it's not first the content or the doctrine that dumbs down, but rather the process of indoctrination.

Same thing happens in school. It dumbs down our kids like it did dumb us down. That we like it or not, we, you and me brothers, have been dumbed down by our schools and our religion!

How does school, with all its good intentions and good reputation dumb people down? It's too involved to be explained at length here, but I just published a book on the dumbing down end result of school called: *Coercion: The Achilles' Heel of Education.*

In brief I tried to demonstrate that, whatever the curriculum of a school, it does dumb down our kids. It has little to do with the curriculum and everything to do with the imposed model of education and the atmosphere of the classroom, i.e. the spirit in which it's delivered and the type of relationship between the teacher and the child. "School does not educate; *it **indoctrinates***. That's a whole different ball game!

"All indoctrination, whatever its content, or the doctrines it proclaims, dumbs people down. How do religion and school succeed to do it in most cases? With the magic ingredient known as coercion"!

That school uses coercion is a given. But if, by any chance, you're a religious person and have the courage to read this book, you will scream at me *that your church doesn't use coercion!!!* Why I call it the best invention of all, business wise, is that to succeed and amass fortunes like the Catholic Church and many others have done, you don't have to be smart or knowledgeable of business practices etc. All you need to know, is how to appeal to the weakness of poor insecure people, to know that the mind of people can be manipulated by acting on their beliefs. By removing from them the right to think, to judge, to decide anything other than what they have been told to believe, *under the threat of the fire from hell,* you have a business …or what some people call a religion.

Now, I have enough on my plate with the Catholic religion, I will not talk about other religions even if some of what I say about the Catholic religion might also apply to them… I'll have the privilege to talk about *"my religion"* at length. And I'll do it with all the honesty I can muster. I won't have to lie or invent anything. That religion has bequeathed me a large inventory of its *"modus operandi"* and of its nooks and crannies.

Mario Jorge, my brother, you have probably guessed that this book will be for me a chance to express what we were not allowed to express while under its spell. I will try to expose this religion *-or cult gone awry-* for many reasons. For me, first, and for my mother who wanted "TWO" kids, as she told me in answer to my asking. She lived *through 18 pregnancies* and slaved for 35 years because of her adherence to a ''certain religion''...

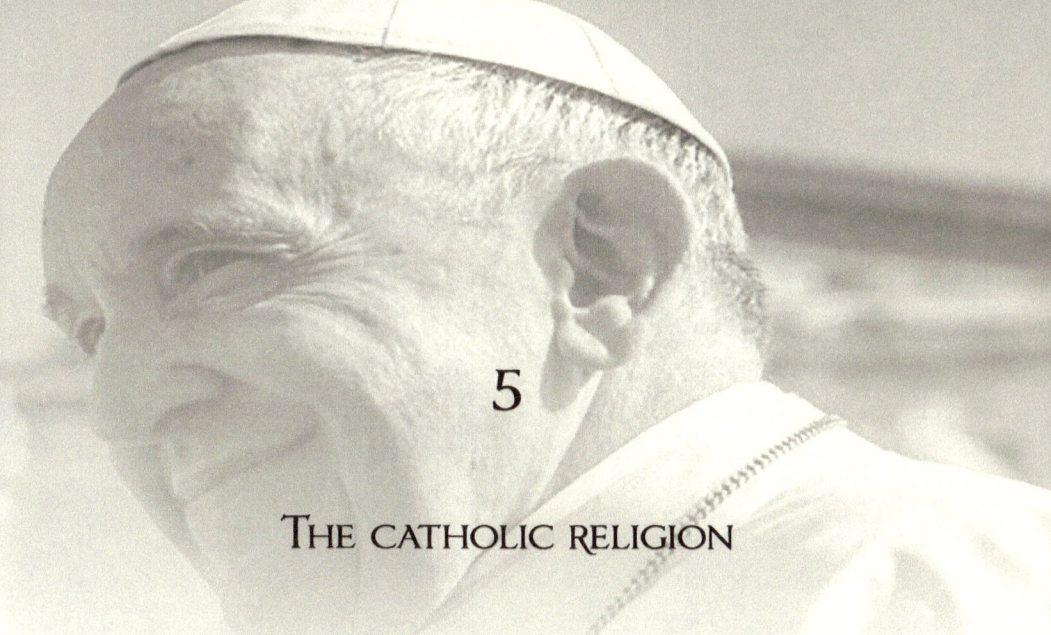

5

The catholic religion

"This is my simple religion. There is no need for temples; no need for complicated philosophy. Our own brain, our own heart is our temple; the philosophy is kindness."

Dalai Lama

In case you might get the idea that I'm against religions, Mario Jorge, my brother, ...well! I am! But only against the power seeking gimmicks some people call religions. And the best example I could choose is the Catholic religion. By the time I'm finished with my critical examination of that religion, I think you will understand why I condemn that religion in particular.

If we look up the word catholic, we find that it comes from the Greek word *katholikos*, meaning: universal. For those of you who didn't know that it means universal, it must be a deception. Because with all the pretention of that religion one would tend to think that it means *"holy or godly"* with some air of grandeur! But the choice of the word universal is easily understandable when we remind ourselves of their ambition and thirst for worldly power and their goal of monopolizing God... Not my words! Their words about being *"the only true religion*

15

of God!". The catholic religion, preaching that it's the only *true* religion, did not start with the birth or the death of Jesus. "Jesus didn't start any religion." For what it's worth, here is my theory.

Let's go back before *"Peter, Paul and …Mary…"* It could have been in the year 10 BC. An alien vessel like the one Ezekiel saw and describes in the Bible, landed in the area of Nazareth and proceeded to tell some chosen people that their lord or king had landed among them. He is coming to visit them and he would like to have a son from a human woman… The ETs give them a precise time when that will take place and where. The ET entities choose a certain type of young girl that is healthy and compatible with the plan of the god. They also instruct her parents to raise her with special care *(vitamins? tonics? drugs? diet?)* and that they will come back when she is of a certain age. Ten years later, Mary is of nubile age. They take her in their vessel (ufo) and they (the doctors) perform an *in vitro* fertilization "with the god's semen???" They remind her parents or keepers to make sure she follows her regimen of magic potions *(hormones, medications vitamins, diet ?)* as prescribed.

Nine months later, on schedule, Mary gave birth to the Lord, the son of the god who came from Heaven to save the human race. The Lord is the son of the sperm donor, god, who sent the ghost, (the doctor) to perform the *in vitro* fertilization. Thus Mary got pregnant by the operation of the ghost (doctor), which in time got elevated to the rank of Holy Ghost.

The 3 Wise Men (or magicians) arrived following the astrological directions they were given by their celestial visitors, carrying precious gifts and possibly hormones and vitamins for mom and little baby Jesus. These gifts and super supplements for mother and child were provided by "god the father". The name Jesus means to save, deliver or delivery, or the savior of the world.

Now it is very easy for anyone, like me, for example, to write any theory and try to have people swallow it. Be assured. I cannot and will not try to indoctrinate you as we have all been at one time or another in our life. This is only a scenario of what *might* have happened. It's only an hypothesis, although I believe it is, ten times more plausible than the shameful plagiarism they did of the then popular Mithraic religions.

Do not believe anything I say. This is not *the* truth; this is *my* truth, *my* hypothesis and the truth about me. What I say, I believe, and it's up to you, and to you alone, to deal with it as you see fit. But if you have a moment, just look up the Mithraic religion. You're in for a gigantic surprise -that you'll probably refuse to believe,- because *it came from the web!* But it has irrefutable historical basis backed by archeological findings. And guess where it had its head office, of all places? According to Wikipedia, "they met in underground temples (called mithraea), which survive in large numbers. The cult appears to have had its centre in Rome. Numerous archeological finds, including meeting places, monuments, and artifacts, have contributed to modern knowledge about Mithraism throughout the Roman Empire."

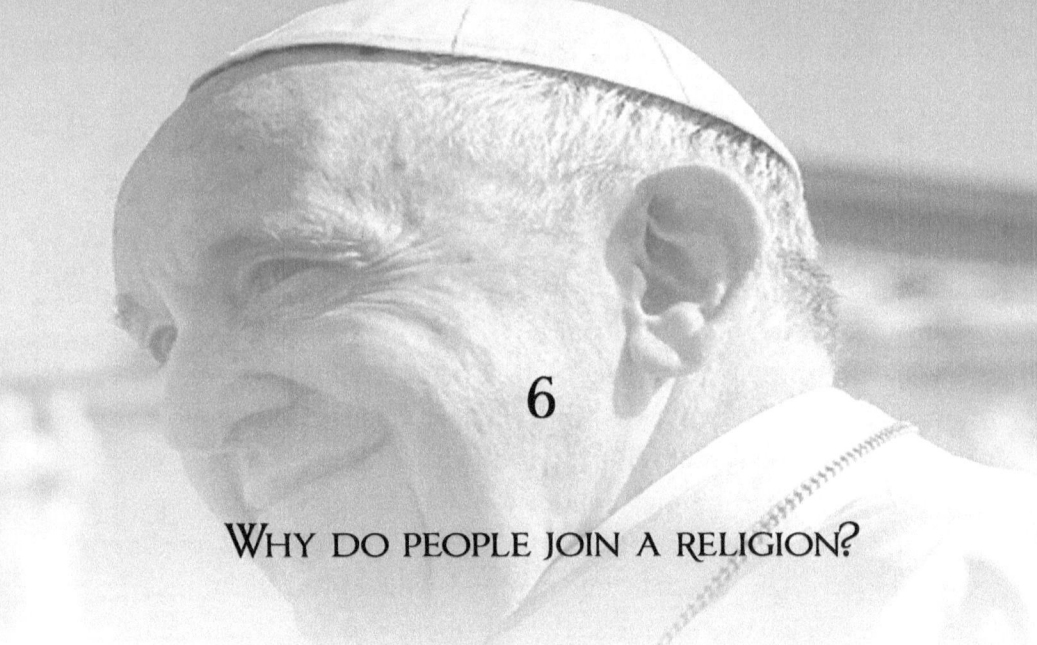

6

WHY DO PEOPLE JOIN A RELIGION?

"The average man is a conformist, accepting miseries and disasters with the stoicism of a cow standing in the rain."

Colin Wilson

Why do people join religions? To be honest with you, I don't know!!! *Maybe they like the rain...*

It's a big question for which I have a very short answer. Ultimately, it's because of fear of death and of the afterlife.

For me, to join a religion shows ...*a lack of faith in God!*

End of chapter!

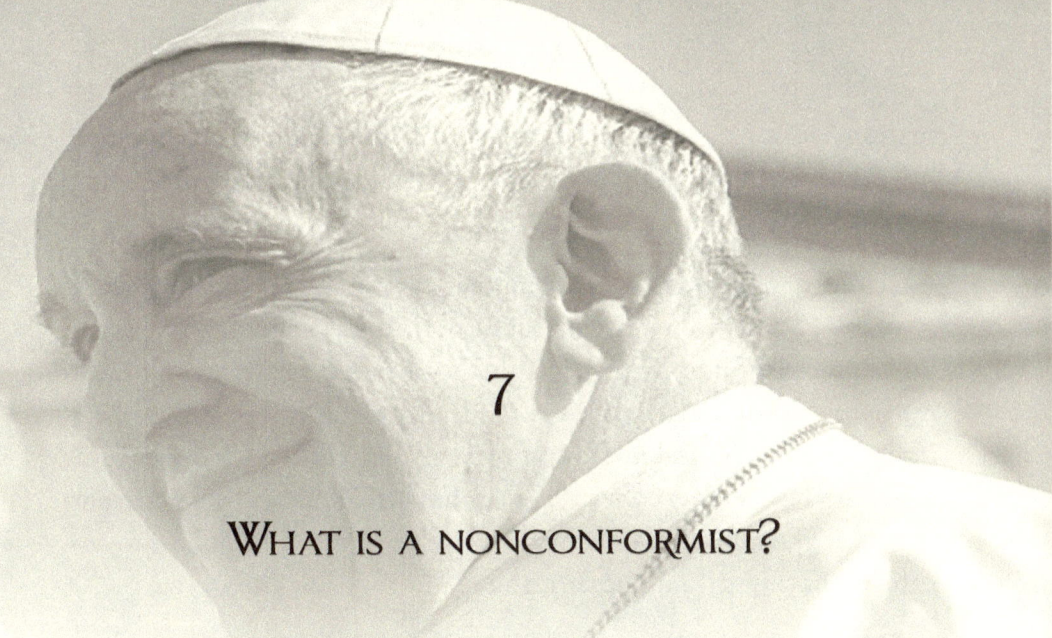

7

WHAT IS A NONCONFORMIST?

"The individual has always had to struggle to keep from being overwhelmed by the tribe. If you try it, you will be lonely often, and sometimes frightened. But no price is too high to pay for the privilege of owning yourself."

Friedrich Nietzsche

If you look up the definition of the word *nonconformist* in Wikipedia you get this: *"a person whose behavior or views do not conform to prevailing ideas or practices."*

If you look closely at the people society calls eccentrics, dissidents, anarchists, revolutionaries, Mario Jorge Bergoglio …Roméos, etc. you will probably find that most of them are nonconformists.

Society is scared of what those individuals who dare to think, *think about*, and by extension, it feels threatened by any person or persons who dare to think. Probably as many as 6 billion people on earth are scared of the opinions of the 15-20% of the individuals among them who are nonconformists. How much threatened can they be? In 99.99% of the cases, the nonconformist doesn't carry any arms of mass destruction, machine guns ...*or even sling shots!* Most of the time the only weapon he's carrying is only an opinion different from theirs! How threatening can that be?

From a nonconformist to another, Mario Jorge, my brother, I must tell you that, for reasons I don't quite understand, I have been a nonconformist for as long as I can remember. My first nonconformist move was to abandon my courses in Pedagogy at the Montréal University in December 1960 and not to complete my degree. The reason for such a *"dumb move"* was my conviction that the curriculum was not pertinent to pedagogy, and was not helping the teacher in me to learn how to co-parent kids. I quit...and never regretted it.

My second really consequential nonconformist move was my *dumping* the catholic religion in 1963. One Sunday, during mass, I was getting ready to stand up in the church and give a piece of my mind to the preacher, in the middle of his sermon. My wife, aware of my feelings at their boiling point, took my arm and said: **"I think we better go..."**

And she was right. I could not continue to pretend that everything was rosy. I'm not against bordellos selling sex, but... I am adamantly against a religion forcing you to prostitute yourself and, in the process, having you *pay them ...for screwing you up!* Now for those of you who are wondering what was the preacher talking about to get a person as patient as myself, out of himself, to the point of risking excommunication...I'm glad you asked. We were in one of the ostentatious churches downtown Montréal and we had arrived late for some reason. The sermon had already begun. The preacher was talking about money. What's new! When, 20 minutes later, he was still talking, that would have been enough to have me sigh... But that he was still talking about money, didn't sit well with me! And what I was preparing myself to tell him was this: *"Hey! Mister Minister of Finance, if and when I want to hear about money, I'll go and see my accountant; not come to church and listen to you!"*

The third time was when I started teaching and realized that the school system, far from having evolved since the days of my school years, had become a governmental concentration camp of sort. The atmosphere had become more and more impersonal. Students were like numbers lost in a sea of bodies looking for their next classroom *like cows looking for their stall in a barn...* The higher the density of a population, the more stressing it becomes for people. When a certain space is not provided around humans, like with any other animals, it creates a certain stress and can even arouse aggressiveness. But let us not jump ahead of ourselves...

People aren't automatically crazy and dangerous because they are nonconformists or smarts and safes because they're conformists. I don't think there's a correlation between the intelligence level among conformists versus that of nonconformists.

Although, I believe it's easier to brainwash a conformist person into becoming a *cult follower* than it is to do the same with a nonconformist. The conformist person has been, and -in most cases-still is... indoctrinated. Indoctrination implies brainwashing. The nonconformist might have been indoctrinated by his family, his school and his church, but at some point, he realized he was not free and dumped the content of his indoctrination and the source of his indoctrination, in most cases, his religion and the ambient culture.

Here, I will have to put myself under the microscope, and let you see how a nonconformist (me) operates... but not you, my brother; you already know...

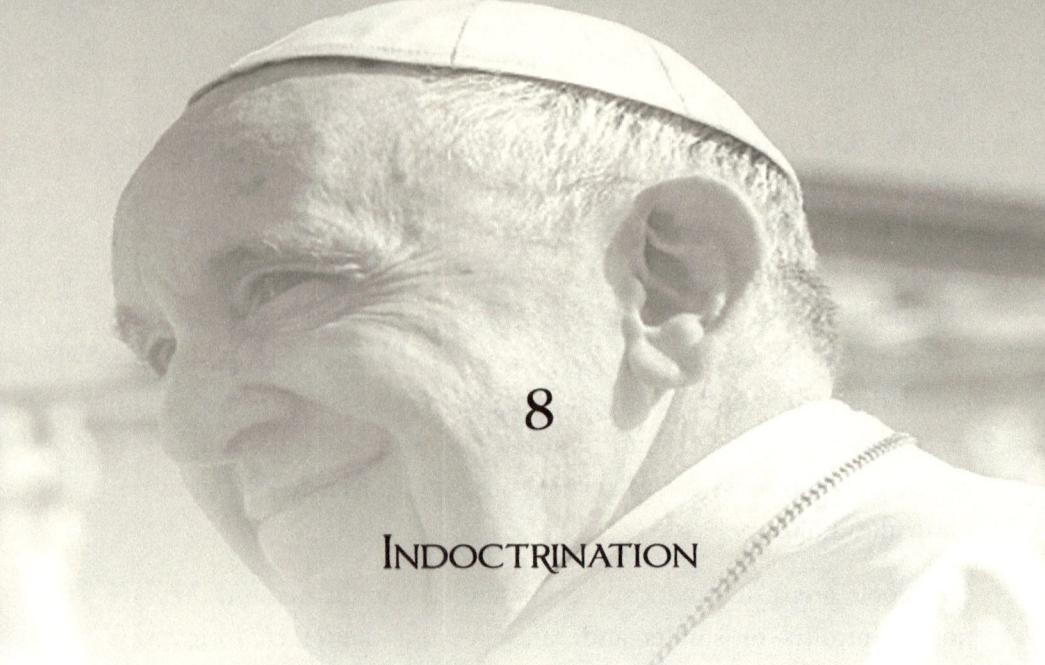

8

INDOCTRINATION

"To terrify children with the image of hell, to consider women an inferior creation—is that good for the world?"

Christopher Hitchens

I was raised in a very catholic family (I was the fifteenth child, *duh!*). I should love the Catholic religion who forced my mother to have me, *as her eighteenth pregnancy!*

Indoctrination is a word that will come back often in this exchange with you. I'll be talking about indoctrination in church and in school, mainly. It isn't the only places where we find it; but those are the places where we find it most. I'll address its strong presence in school where it's used basically for the same reasons: to condition and to shape people in a certain desired configuration.

If we believe Wikipedia, *"indoctrination is the process of inculcating ideas, attitudes, cognitive strategies or a professional methodology. …It is often distinguished from education, by the fact that the indoctrinated person is expected not to question or critically examine the doctrine they have learned."* I couldn't have said it better

22

myself! Doesn't it resume the *"modus operandi"* of the Church and of the school to a T? … *"that the indoctrinated person is expected not to question or critically examine the doctrine they have learned."*

I would add to this: nor the way or the atmosphere in which it was delivered. In the case of the Catholic religion, it was not expected; it was imposed under the threat of hell. And Wikipedia adds: *"As such, the term may be used pejoratively, often in the context of education, political opinions, theology or religious dogma. The term is closely linked to socialization."*

May be used pejoratively!!! I'm tempted to say: **Duh!** If we make the connection between indoctrination and socialization, we open a whole can of worms with incredible possibilities and advantages for the establishment. That is the main reason why the governments put up with Churches from behind the scene. These Churches "socialize" people…

If you allow me, I will expand on the word "socialize" and give it an injection of realism and define its all-encompassing meaning. When organizations like governments, Churches (not all) and school socialize their clientele, they funnel them through a funnel/sieve contraption to make them fit the *status quo*. The *status quo* is composed of systems and people that have passed through the funnel/sieve of government, Church and school. I could certainly add of the family, but that'll be for later.

*"**The intellectual tradition is one of servility to power, and if I didn't betray it I'd be ashamed of myself.**"*

Noam Chomsky

Any time you indoctrinate people, you have a goal in mind. And that goal is **never** to the advantage of the person being indoctrinated, whatever your motivation might be. The goal is to condition, control and use the victim to the advantage of a given system. Most of the time the goal is capitalist or political, but it boils down to one thing: *power!* Gain of power, increase of power or the maintaining of power. Power is one of the biggest things coveted by a certain number of people ...or rather a number of certain people. Everybody wants power. Everybody *needs* a certain amount of power to survive and achieve certain goals. Those are examples of normal wants for power.

Indoctrination is a word for which I have lots of feelings. Mostly feelings of contempt for what it did to me, to my mother, and to the great majority of women of my mother's generation who were morally forced to conceive children as many times as nature would allow them to, without having the choice to say no. They had the choice, but they didn't feel they were entitled mentally, emotionally, intellectually and spiritually to tell *"the parish priest where to go"* and do anything in their power to avoid pregnancies, even refusing intercourse, when they had enough kids...if it came to that!

When someone talks about events that happened three quarters of a century ago, and that he attended these events, Mario Jorge my brother, he's no spring chicken ...*or he's lying!* Well, I was there...sort off! My mother, who already had twelve children, was blessed with my arrival... I was her **eighteenth** pregnancy! Obviously, there was a part of birth control she didn't understand... or was there? In 1938, for the French people in Quebec, there was nothing to understand! There was no birth control, or any control for that matter ...other than the almighty control: *the control by the Catholic Church.* You were not allowed to think, to judge, to analyze, to decide or to use any other mental function of yours with regard to their teachings. The Church was telling you *why* to think, *when* to think, *what* to think about, *how* to think...and most often ...not to think! ...*And more!*

She was born in Carleton, Quebec, about twelve kilometers from Nouvelle. She was born from strong roots. Her father, Paul Caron, was known to be the strongest man around... and maybe the strongest man in the world!

"The family is both the fundamental unit of society as well as the root of culture. It is a perpetual source of encouragement, *advocacy, assurance, and emotional refueling that empowers a child to venture with confidence into the greater world and to become all that he can be.*"

MARIANNE E. NEIFERT, Dr. Mom's Parenting Guide

9

SCHOOL

S chool is probably the most influential life experience that we go through in our life. And wanting to be closer to the truth, I'll rephrase that sentence: school is probably the most influential life experience *that we have no choice ... but to go through, in our life.*

Instead of rehashing what I just wrote in a book I published in August 2014, I thought I would reproduce it here for your delight... (I have a minute ego...)
I hope you'll enjoy reading it as much as I enjoyed writing it.

Coercion: The Achilles' Heel of Education (from this author.)

Chapter 3, Coercion and compulsory schooling.

"I think schools generally do an effective and terribly damaging job of teaching children to be infantile, dependent, intellectually dishonest, passive and disrespectful to their own developmental capacities."

Seymour Papert

When we are told that our state's or our province's schools compare well enough with the schools of other industrialized countries, what does that really mean? It means that the academic performance of our schools is equal to –or greater than–that of most industrialized countries.

"Our School Report Cards offer detailed tables showing how well schools performed in academics over a number of years. By combining a variety of relevant objective indicators ... (we) compare the academic performance of individual schools..."

(www.fraser institute.org)

For me, when the only thing we can brag about, regarding our school system, is academics, I'm very deceived! In my scale of values, academics are far from being at the top of the list. Here's what I would like our School Report Card analysts to understand and to take into consideration:

A school system that is first in academics and second or third, in respect of the student, in the quality of relation of the teacher with the student, in its degree of cohesion with the students, in its non-coercive approach with the students, and finally, a school system that is first in academics and second or third in its understanding of the all-embracing vocation of co-parenting the students doesn't deserve the name of school.

In the present system, we force our kids to go to school. By law, in America, schooling is compulsory from age 6 to 16. Most will agree that there is nothing wrong with going to school and getting an education. If the school delivers that education without abusing the kids, it seems reasonable enough to send the kids to school. My task will be to find out if the school delivers the much coveted education it promises, and if it uses coercion in the process. And, if so, what are the psychological, social and spiritual fallouts on our kids.

I'm sure, Mario Jorge, my brother, that I don't have to explain to you what coercion is. But let's still look at a definition of coercion on

Wikipedia: *"In law, coercion is codified as a duress crime. Such actions … to force the victims to act in a way contrary to their own interests. The threat of further harm may lead to the cooperation or obedience of the person being coerced."*

This part of the definition: "…to force the victim to act in a way contrary to their own interests" is pivotal here to understand the ramifications of compulsory/coercive schooling. For all purposes, in this case, the victims are the students. I see them as victims by the fact that mostly, they are not there by choice. A high percentage of them are there against their will, by the force of the compulsory schooling law, and by the pressure of the parents enforcing that law and forcing them to go. This is an example of parental coercion. There are many others as we will see. How could it be contrary to their own interest?

The answer to that short but extremely volatile question is, I maintain, contained in my book I just told you about and that hopefully you might end up holding in your hands one day.

"Do not train a child to learn by force or harshness; but direct them to it by what amuses their minds, so that you may be better able to discover with accuracy the peculiar bent of the genius of each."

Plato (348-428 BC…)

Basically everybody knows of Plato and how wise a philosopher he was. He lived over 2400 years ago and his philosophy still makes more sense than the one of most of today's philosophers… He left us with a lot of wisdom. We use some of it in our everyday conversations. These pearls are an example of it:

"*Necessity* is the mother of invention." And: "*Beauty lies*" in the eyes of the beholder", and many more.

He clearly means that we can't transmit knowledge to people while using coercion. We can force them to sit quiet and pretend to listen; but that's all!

In my attempt to demonstrate that school uses coercion as a way of controlling the students and forcing them into obedience, which is a form of subjugation, –short of saying a form of bullying– I will try to be fair to teachers and school principals. I will try to underline the fact that the principals and the teachers are caught in the iron grips of a system designed over 150 years ago by a government that had training in mind; *not education!* That was the legalization of compulsory schooling by the American government, which was adopted by Canada not long after.

We must remember that teaching is a government job and that the school system is a government department and that the school boards are satellite governments, each administering the schools of their district. By reading the next quote, Mario Jorge my brother, you'll find out what I really think of the school boards...

"In the first place God made idiots. That was for practice. Then he made school boards."

Mark Twain

Because of the nature of compulsory schooling, we can observe... "the act of coercing, use of force or intimidation to obtain compliance..." The use of force is less and less frequent than it was in my time, but it still exists in lots of countries "The use of intimidation to obtain compliance" on the other hand is the backbone of our school system, (of some of our churches,) and of all governments, military and policing forces in the world. And one cannot talk about coercion without talking about power, *from the prime minister down to the single parent.*

"Power may comprise anything that establishes and maintains the control of man over man. Thus power covers all social relationships,

which serve that end, from physical violence to the most subtle psychological ties by which one mind controls another."

Hans Morgenthau

What can we do about coercion in our society? I'm not sure that realistically we can force the establishment to change the rules of their game. For one, to force them would require coercion, which we're trying to convince them to abstain from... It would be self-defeating and illogical. In that sense, although I think our governments are corrupted, I believe we should replace them with true democratic governments. But we should not do it by way of a coup, a revolution, a civil war or any kind of coercion. Coercion never produces positive results! The only way to have a democratic government one day is for us to change ourselves and when enough of us will no longer be subjugated and victims of indoctrination from any source whatsoever, be it the family, the school, the Church, the government or any socio-cultural entity, *then –and perhaps only then–* will we have a chance at a true democracy.

We are not victims of those indoctrinations. We are born into their powerful tentacles, but we choose to remain victims instead of taking back our human dignity and to unknot those tentacles which restrain us from growing! A country can't invade another country under the pretext that it is going there to bring them democracy. I would rather try, by education, to de-program people at the bottom of the chain of command,–you and me– from the indoctrination we have been subjected to throughout our whole life.

And one of the ways to realize that goal is to help people realize that we have *all* been indoctrinated and coerced from a very young age, by all of our sacred institutions, family included, in most cases. And we achieve that by refusing to be the recipients of any more indoctrination, would it be from the Queen, our prime minister or the *Pope!* Eventually, it would bring about a great societal renewal of these institutions, of our role in society and in the level of respect of self and of others we would reach.

Writing books on the subject, writing blogs and posts on the internet could, to some degree, help us educate and inform ourselves and others on the issue of coercion and its capital role in the derailing of human affairs on the path to re-civilization.

It took the school, the Church and the government over 2,000 years to subjugate people to this extreme. Reversing the steam will not happen overnight! But if we don't try, millions of our kids will continue to be victims of coercive indoctrination, via educational mumbo jumbo. So, for me, the school is the first place where to start, with the collaboration of the parents.

"There is no greater insight into the future than recognizing... when we save our children, we save ourselves"

Margaret Mead

It will be an uphill battle against the culture but I don't know of any other way or any other place where to start than in the school.

One day, around 1880, while Edison was trying to find a better filament for his incandescent light bulb, one of his helpers told him:

"Mr. Edison, you have tried over a 1000 times to find a proper filament and failed. Don't you think you should give up?"

Mr. Edison replied:

"I now know a 1000 ways that don't work. I should find the right way very soon."

And as the story goes, the next trial was successful. So we have to keep trying because it's as worthy a cause as we can possibly tackle, and also because helping our fellow man is helping us both to self-actualize in the great school of life where the soul's journey is more important than money, power, and mundane success combined!

> *"A child whose life is full of the threat and fear of punishment is locked into babyhood. There is no way for him to grow up, to learn to take responsibility for his life and acts."*

John Holt

End of chapter 3 from: *Coercion: The Achilles' Heel of Education*

You must wonder, Mario Jorge, my brother, why I chose to include this chapter on the school in a book on religion. For those who might not see the link, here it is. School, like religion, indoctrinates. And to make possible this indoctrination, compulsory schooling for children 6 to 16 years old became law over 100 years ago. And to keep control over the children, the school uses coercion or constraint.

Religious education indoctrinates parents who, in turn, indoctrinate their children and the school completes the circle. All this indoctrination dumbs down and conditions children into a life of servility. You might not like what follows, my friend, but there was lots of stuff I didn't like when I was young and a victim of the Vatican orders about indoctrination, or more honestly, about brainwashing, but I had no choice!

You can, if you really want to, just turn the page or put my book away. *I didn't have such options!* But it's not you I should tell these things to. You understand; you're not a conformist *like somebody we both know…* We were asked to lie to ourselves mentally by pretending to believe what we didn't believe, like the pseudo miracles of the Catholic religion. I will use as an example the story of the miracles of Fatima. It's a childish story with absolutely no proofs whatsoever of any kind of verifiable facts. To me, it looks very opportunistic on the part of the Church of the time. But it's only my opinion. What do I know?

10

CONDITIONING TO CONTROL

"It will, of course, be understood that directly or indirectly, soon or late, every advance in the sciences of human nature will contribute to our success in controlling human nature and changing it to the advantage of the common weal."

Edward Thorndike

The powers that be, need to control the populations in order to achieve the level of power they thirst for. I'm not telling you anything you don't already know, Mario Jorge my brother. And there are many ways to control people, some more efficient than others. One that appears to be very effective, if we look around us in our country and in the world, is the manipulation of beliefs or a systematic conditioning of the minds from a very young age. Condition a young generation properly and they will in turn condition their offspring and, in doing so, the generations to come. The governments do it, the Churches do it, the school does it, and so do families, some more than others.

"When it comes to controlling human beings, there is no better instrument than lies. Because you see, humans live by beliefs. And

beliefs can be manipulated. The power to manipulate beliefs is the only thing that counts

Michael Ende

When people refuse to question their institutions, they are putting their kids' and their own welfare in danger. We should be skeptical when our destiny is in other people's hands, especially when we realize that lots of the people who are in posts of command are power hungry, egomaniacs, when they're not purely and simply sociopaths. Those are strong accusations and I'm aware of it.

"Education has failed in a very serious way to convey the most important lesson science can teach: skepticism."

David Suzuki

"If it sounds too good to be true", it usually is. Our school system, in spite of the good intentions of most teachers, does not deliver what it could or what it should. It has been created to condition the future citizens. A dumbed down population is much easier to control and predict. And, because it has been conditioned to believe what it's told, a dumbed down population, given the appropriate indoctrination, will do what it has been programmed to do, in a high percentage of the cases.

You take the strongest living animal, you raise it from a year old with a chain in its leg, like a tether, attached to a post. As it grows, you diminish the size of the chain. After years, you trade the chain for a rope. A big rope at first and you gradually reduce the strength of the rope until you replace the smallest rope with a ribbon that the elephant could break and free itself without effort. What happens then? The elephant remains a prisoner of a symbolic tie. *It's a great illustration of conditioning!!!*

The same thing happens to us, *the most intelligent beings of the creation*, as we like to think... We end up disempowered by our institutions using the most powerful and efficient tool of conditioning known as indoctrination. ***Breaking that ribbon, that tether, is a must if we want to give birth to ourselves and thus become who we're meant to be.***

The remaining percentage of those who have not responded to the conditioning properly, will have to deal with the justice and policing system of the country, which will use convincing means –or coercion– to shut them up, if they dare express opinions different from the establishment's opinions. But let's look at the Almighty Power.

TWILIGHT (CREPUSCULE)

The day is already consumed,

The sun declining far away,

On golden sea, its day resumed,

The horizon, out of the way.

Like the soul of a moribund

That retires in the silence,

Its gently shades of red abound,

On golden sea slowly balances.

Pure gold water seems to swallow

The silent sinking great Monarch,

Without a sound the scene mellows;

The whole nature plunged in the dark

And like the end and the outcome,

Of this drama for mother Earth

Like a curtain, down the night comes,

Thus hiding the sight of the hearth.

Roméo Gauvreau, Feb. 15, 1959,

Translation, Feb. 15, 2013. (Coincidence???)

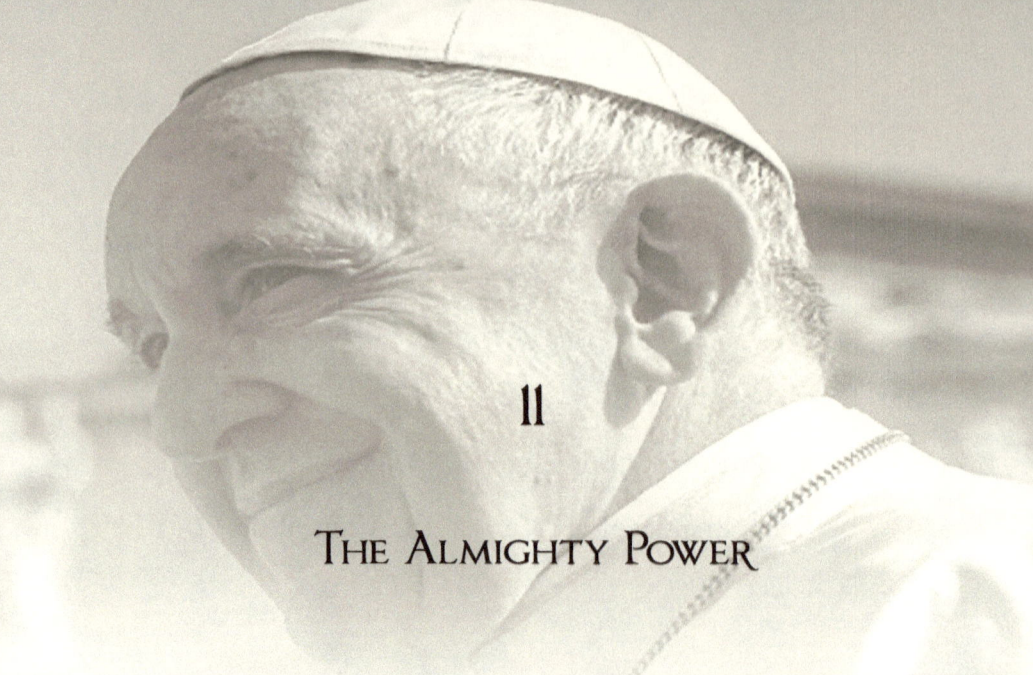

11

THE ALMIGHTY POWER

"Experience hath shown, that even under the best forms of government those entrusted with power have, in time, and by slow operations, perverted it into tyranny."

Thomas Jefferson

The almighty power should be the power of the people or the power of God: ***"Vox populi, vox Dei!"*** or "the voice of the people is the voice of God." But His power is not as tyrannical on earth as the one of His *usurpers* who pretend to be the delegated power of God on earth.

With all due respect, Mario Jorge, my brother, don't you find a bit arrogant that a religion or a person declares that they detain the power of God on earth? Well, the Catholic Church does just that. Doesn't it? The pope is the right hand of God, I've been told. He holds the power of God on His Church, and is ***infallible*** when he talks while sitting on a certain chair they call "***cathedra***". Hence the expression: talking ***"ex cathedra."*** Tell me! Do you believe that???

Now, I'm not very smart, but how could somebody come up with such a fairy tale and try to squeeze it by adults in 2023??? And the Catholic Church proclaims —or used to proclaim— that their path is the only path to heaven... Is it me or does this sound like a story concocted by a 3 year old child ...on Ritalin?

Mind you, Mario Jorge, my brother, I have missed a lot of masses since 1963! Maybe the Church has gotten out of the middle age and has somewhat evolved since my days... I really hope so!

It is probably difficult for the younger generation to understand how we could have been that subjugated by a religion. Well, it was not *a* religion: it was *the* religion, the *only* religion. The Church said so!

12

THE BIBLE

"Properly read, the Bible is the most potent force for atheism ever conceived."

Isaac Asimov

The first time I heard about the Bible, I was still in my mother's womb... Seriously, where I come from, in Gaspé, Québec, people were not allowed to read the bible. Although our church was preaching that it was the word of God, we were forbidden to even possess a Bible! If I translate that strange behavior in 2023 language, it means:

"This book is the most important book ever written. It's been written through God inspired peoples and it's the word of God. But you are not allowed to read it; you might interpret it wrongly. Only **we**, the delegates of God, are smart enough to read it and understand it. Just take our word for it and do what you're told and you'll go to heaven…"

When, finally, I had the opportunity to read it, I understood why they didn't want us to read it, in the first place, I was quite surprised and deceived. I had imagined that a book written by God would be very impressive and *would be accompanied by lightning bolts and thunder.*

I had expected something super different from anything I had read to that day! And it was different. I was literally astounded at the mundane and irrelevant content it was to my life, and to me. It was a collection of stories that had nothing to do with God, other than the additions included in the Bible later on by the Catholic Church and others… I'm sure, at this point, lots of people are wondering why I give you such a hard time, since you're not the bad guy here. Believe me, I have no intention of putting you down.

You are not the Church! You certainly didn't create the wrongs of that Church or commit those irrational actions. You don't seem the type. Far from that! But you're now at the helm of that highly and justly criticized Church. I don't mean to offend you, Mario Jorge my brother, but these things have to be said, these irregularities, these crimes have to be addressed!

You're not God. You're not the inventor of that very questionable cult. And luckily enough, you are the first pope that is giving me hope that the winds are about to change and that the people of the world will finally have the respect and justice they deserve. I, in large part, represent the silent majority of ex-catholics, agnostics, atheists, who can talk about your erratic religion to anybody, but not to you. And that, with no fault of yours. You're just the right man at the right place, at the right time! Believe me, we admire your courage, your down to earth attitude, your humility, your simplicity and your heartfelt sympathy for those who have been wronged.

Your whole Church's doctrine is a blasphemy to God! You (the Church) teaches things about God that are irrevocably wrong, degrading to God, belittling and lowering Him to our level, which is the worst possible blasphemy you have concocted in a million years. Please stop to show yourselves *as being in His close company.* You might think I'm a complete crackpot, Mario Jorge my brother, and maybe I am. But I would feel awful if you thought that any of my attacks on the Church are meant to hurt you by ricochet. I want you to be reassured that what I'm putting down is not the result of who you are and what you did or didn't do. What I'm putting down with deep conviction, are some of the irrational actions of a Church who pretends to be Godly and so right on everything.

You certainly didn't create the wrongs of that Church or commit those irrational actions. Far from that! But you're now at the helm of that highly criticized religion and justly criticized too!

I don't believe in the Bible other than certain verses that might have an historical value. The rest, for me, is just fairy tales when it's not pure cruel stories. If God would ever inspire or write a book (which He would never do, according to my beliefs,) it would be a very short book or letter, meaning something like this:

Hi, loved Children, Co-creators and partners,

"Love and respect yourself, love and respect your fellow man as I love You. Be kind to all and most importantly: Do unto others as You would like them do unto You. I'm proud of You all! Continue the pursuit of discovery of Self, of Others and of Everything around you. …Love, love, love!

Good luck! Children. I love you unconditionally,

Yours always,

As far as those the Church calls prophets, in modern days we call psychics or clairvoyants. Ezekiel was a psychic like Edgar Cayce was. There were others, but I would not say that God talked directly to them or inspired them to say what they said. I never read anything in the Bible that struck me as extraordinary or even divine. It might be a reason to believe for the Catholics, but it doesn't constitute an objective truth. The Bible might be historically true, but certainly not the interpretation they make of it!

Here's a list of some chosen verses for you to meditate on.

In this first verse, Samuel, gives some advice to a leader of Israel:

"This is what the Lord Almighty says... "Now go and strike Amalek and devote to destruction all that they have. Do not spare them, but kill both man and woman, child and infant, ox and sheep, camel and donkey."

(1 Samuel 15:3)

Moses commands his people:

"Do not allow a sorceress to live."

(Exodus 22:18)

No wonder this ending of Psalm 137, is often omitted from readings in church:

"Happy is he who repays you for what you have done to us – he who seizes your infants and dashes them against the rocks."

(Psalm 137:9)

"Wives, submit to your husbands as to the Lord."

(Ephesians 5:22)

"Slaves, submit yourselves to your masters with all respect, not only to the good and gentle but also to the cruel."

(1 Peter 2:18)

P.S.

I would hate to bore you with these *"words of God"*, but let me bring one more to your attention:

"And Jephthah made a vow to the Lord, and said, 'If you will give the Ammonites into my hand, then whoever comes out of the doors of my house to meet me, when I return victorious from the Ammonites, shall be the Lord's, to be offered up by me as a burnt-offering.'

Jephthah came back victorious. His only daughter came out of the house dancing with excitement. He then remembered his vow to God, tore his clothing and said:

"Alas, my daughter! You have brought me very low; you have become the cause of great trouble to me. For I have opened my mouth to the Lord, and I cannot take back my vow."

(Judges 11:30-1, 34-5)

In closing this weird chapter on the Bible, I want to devote a chapter to give you my opinion on what I think really happened. Why does the Bible seem so tasteless, cruel and just a pile of drivel?

I could tell you that the next chapter is probably a pure creation of my imagination. But not wanting to mimic the Catholic Church and ask you to make an act of faith, here is an excerpt of it in the next chapter.

«Perhaps we've never been visited by aliens because they have looked upon Earth and decided there's no sign of intelligent life.»

Neil de Grasse Tyson

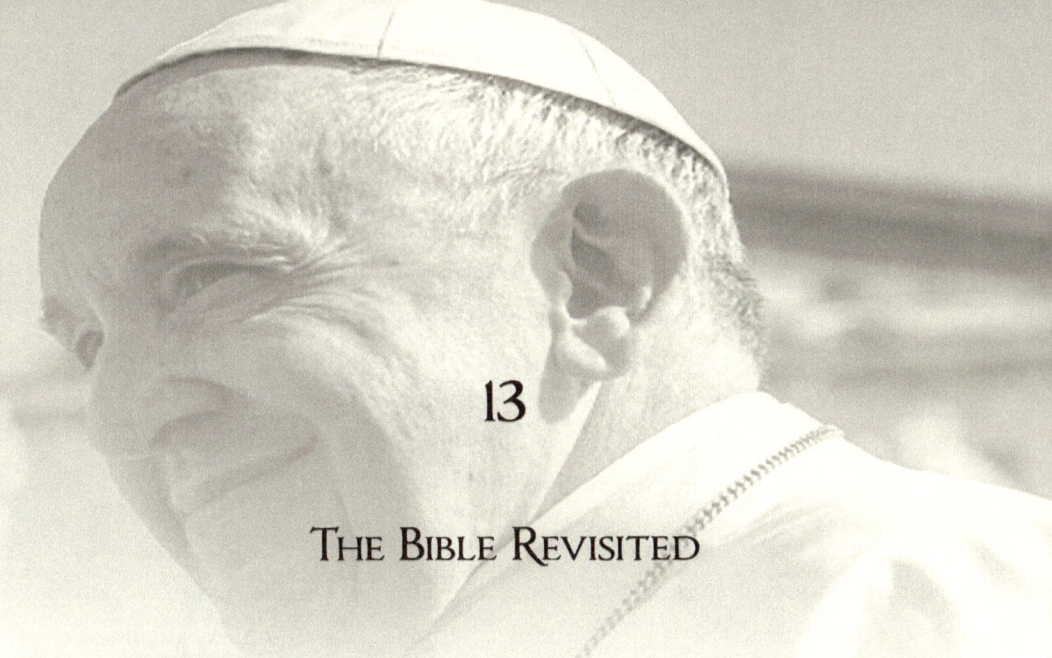

13

The Bible Revisited

"Properly read the bible is the most potent   force for atheism ever conceived"

Isaac Asimov

In all honesty, I do not know who organized the compilation of the bible, nor why or how. My explanation of the phenomenon is that the burgeoning church felt that it needed some kind of credentials… like I needed a PhD that I don't have and I came up with my *Ph.D.… in B.S.!*

In their thirst for recognition and power, they came up with the subterfuge. Impressive for people from the fifth century, but between you and me, in 2023, …it doesn't sound clever... anymore. And don't get me wrong; I'm well aware that probably over 2 billion people say they believe in the Bible. So are the priests who read it hundreds of times and abuse our children sexually, sometime over a period of many years! If that amount of pious reading didn't refrain them from that criminal conduct, can it be that powerful??? Between you and me, I don't understand that people could be that gullible …or hypocritical!

But if I think more rationally, I think it is very possible that the document has a historical value that we could possibly understand and that we could benefit from if the document had not very likely, been modified. There are numerous arguments saying that, over the ages, the Church could have made it say what it wanted it to say. And it gave it (the Church) great importance and made it seem like the chosen Church of God, the only true Church. In that sense, the Bible could have been manipulated and could possibly have lost an incommensurable historical value! Please, let me explain.

Either the Bible is a compilation of worthless drivel for those who are not indoctrinated and in part, bordering on science fiction, or, on the other hand, the Bible was not a religious document at all, but a historical document out of the ordinary and very important. I believe the Bible could have report incredible and incomprehensible events for people of the time. I believe that often, without understanding what they reported, they reported what they had seen and heard without words to express it in a scientific or technological way. Could they have seen aliens coming down from heaven, where, normally, only God and the angels live? And if so, what would they have said or written???

One day, about 25 or 30 years ago, I came across a part of the Bible that surprised me a lot, at first, and then gave me great pleasure. Not often in my life, have I associated the words Bible and pleasure in the same sentence... But this time, I came across a very revealing passage in the bible. It was a testimony of Ezekiel, who lived about 600 years before Jesus. Here's that testimony we hear very little about in church ...and for good reasons!

Sorry to bore you, Mario Jorge my brother, with that document you probably know by heart, but that my readers might not be familiar with. I won't be insulted if you skip the next three pages...

Extract from the New International Version, Ezekiel's inaugural vision.

"In my thirtieth year, in the fourth month on the fifth day, while I was among the exiles by the Kebar River, the heavens were opened and I saw visions of God. I looked, and I saw a windstorm coming out of the north— an immense cloud with flashing lightning and surrounded by brilliant light. The center of the fire looked like glowing metal, and in the fire was what looked like four living creatures. In appearance their form was human, but each of them had four faces and four wings. Their legs were straight; their feet were like those of a calf and gleamed like burnished bronze. Under their wings on their four sides they had human hands. All four of them had faces and wings, and the wings of one touched the wings of another. Each one went straight ahead; they did not turn as they moved.

Their faces looked like this: Each of the four had the face of a human being, and on the right side each had the face of a lion, and on the left the face of an ox; each also had the face of an eagle. Such were their faces. They each had two wings spreading out upward, each wing touching that of the creature on either side; and each had two other wings covering its body. Each one went straight ahead. Wherever the spirit would go, they would go, without turning as they went. The appearance of the living creatures was like burning coals of fire or like torches. Fire moved back and forth among the creatures; it was bright, and lightning flashed out of it. The creatures sped back and forth like flashes of lightning.

As I looked at the living creatures, I saw a wheel on the ground beside each creature with its four faces. This was the appearance and structure of the wheels: They sparkled like topaz, and all four looked alike. Each appeared to be made like a wheel intersecting a wheel. As they moved, they would go in any one of the four directions the creatures faced; the wheels did not change direction as the creatures went.

Their rims were high and awesome, and all four rims were full of eyes all around.

When the living creatures moved, the wheels beside them moved; and when the living creatures rose from the ground, the wheels also rose. Wherever the spirit would go, they would go, and the wheels would rise along with them, because the spirit of the living creatures was in the wheels. When the creatures moved, they also moved; when the creatures stood still, they also stood still; and when the creatures rose from the ground, the wheels rose along with them, because the spirit of the living creatures was in the wheels.

Spread out above the heads of the living creatures was what looked something like a vault, sparkling like crystal, and awesome. Under the vault their wings were stretched out one toward the other, and each had two wings covering its body. When the creatures moved, I heard the sound of their wings, like the roar of rushing waters, like the voice of the Almighty, like the tumult of an army. When they stood still, they lowered their wings.

Then there came a voice from above the vault over their heads as they stood with lowered wings. Above the vault over their heads was what looked like a throne of lapis lazuli, and high above on the throne was a figure like that of a man. I saw that from what appeared to be his waist up he looked like glowing metal, as if full of fire, and that from there down he looked like fire; and brilliant light surrounded him. Like the appearance of a rainbow in the clouds on a rainy day, so was the radiance around him.

This was the appearance of the likeness of the glory of the LORD. When I saw it, I fell facedown, and I heard the voice of one speaking.

Ezekiel's Call to Be a Prophet

He said to me, **"Son of man, stand up on your feet and I will speak to you."** *As he spoke, the Spirit came into me and raised me to my feet, and I heard him speaking to me.*

He said: **"Son of man, I am sending you to the Israelites, to a rebellious nation that has rebelled against me; they and their ancestors have been in revolt against me to this very day. The people to whom I am sending you are obstinate and stubborn. Say to them, 'This is what the Sovereign LORD says.' And whether they listen or fail to listen—for they are a rebellious people—they will know that a** *prophet has been among them. And you, son of man, do not be afraid of them or their words. Do not be afraid, though briers and thorns are all around you and you live among scorpions. Do not be afraid of what they say or be terrified by them, though they are a rebellious people. You must speak my words to them, whether they listen or fail to listen, for they are rebellious. But you, son of man, listen to what I say to you. Do not rebel like that rebellious people; open your mouth and eat what I give you."*

Then I looked, and I saw a hand stretched out to me. In it was a scroll, which he unrolled before me. On both sides of it were written words of lament and mourning and woe."

Ezekiel's Inaugural Vision, Ezekiel 12

I can't tell you for sure what it means, but here's what I think. He is without a doubt describing one or many flying machines. This flying machine, very likely was an alien flying vessel of some sort.

It may well be that this visit from some extraterrestrial visitor(s), had also happened many times before and would happen again later. That would very well explain all the times, in the Bible, when they speak of the Lord or the son of God (son of the god???), promising to help them improve their primitive ignorant lives. If it came from the sky, had wings and were surrounded by fire (rocket flames), for them, it had to be a messenger of God, or God Himself.

Anyway, we're talking about people who had no concepts or words with which they could understand and explain these phenomena which are overwhelming even for us in 2023! What Ezekiel wrote is, I think, a valuable historical document, valuable because he did not comprehend what he was saying when he wrote it, neither did the Church who would have removed it from the Bible as it has apparently removed and changed many things to embellish their stories …or not contradict them. Those are conjectures, not God's truth.

49

The Bible shows the way to go to heaven, not the way the heavens go.

Galileo Galilei

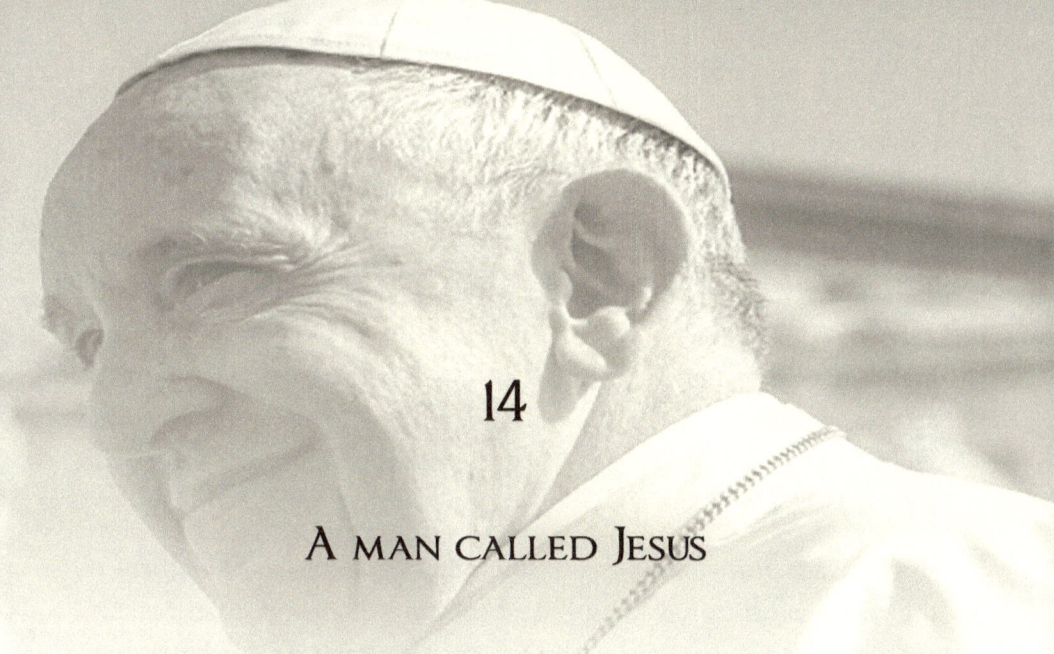

14

A MAN CALLED JESUS

"Jesus is ideal and wonderful, but you Christians you are not like him."

Mahatma Gandhi

Jesus doesn't need any introduction. Everyone knows who I mean. I must specify here that I do not speak of Jesus "the Christ." I'm talking about Jesus, "the man". Jesus *the Christ*, for me, represents something different from the Catholic Church interpretation. One thing I believe, though, he must have been a very advanced soul to have left such a deep imprint on the last two millennia. But, as usual, I have opinions about Jesus that are far from being conformist or traditionalist.

First, Mario Jorge, my brother, I don't see the need of God sending a messenger to tell the world how to live and what to do and die on a cross for their sins. In my way of seeing the creation, if there is a god, He is perfect. Perfection implies many attributes. In no particular order, He would be infinitely powerful. He would be infinitely good. He would be infinitely intelligent, and infinitely forgiving. He would be infinitely self-confident, i.e. he wouldn't need our worshipping or our pious ramblings (prayers). In a word, He would be perfectly everything in accordance with the Law, *His Law!*

Being a perfect God, he would have created man and the universe and, possibly, a lot more we're not aware of, and would have created it perfectly. In that way, man is a perfect creature in evolution towards a higher degree of perfection. God planned the way a man should be, according to his desire, his vision *and maybe his sense of humor... Ha! Ha!* I hope he designed man out of his sense of humor... Otherwise, *we're kaput!!! Ha! Ha!*

So God created man and all the other creatures and put them on the planet earth, for sure, and maybe ...on millions of other "earths". We don't know. That would be for another book on ETs! We know NOTHING about the universe! I'll come back in time to treat of what we know and of what we think we know.

The story of God sending His son Jesus on earth to take the load of sins of men on his shoulders and die on the cross to save mankind, presents a few logistic problems to my feeble mind.

Yeah! Mario Jorge my brother, I'm aware of the magnitude of the following of Jesus, being around 2 billion, close to 30% of the earth's population. I believe we are talking about one of the most influential people the earth has ever known. I get that. But I don't believe in the Christ part or his persona making him part of the Trinity. When I hear that God gave us His only begotten son, I shake my head in disbelief! If God created us, all of us, how could he tell us that he preferred this one to the rest of all his other sons and daughters in the creation???

Maybe I'm not a scholar, but if I would tell one of my two sons that he is *my begotten son,* the other one would look at me funny and probably tell me where to go ...and I would deserve it. It's unbelievable how indoctrinated people can create such scenarios, believe them to be true and inspired by God and convince the masses that it's the truth, the only truth and nothing but the truth...! And most surprisingly, they find hundreds of millions of people to believe it! It's all science fiction anyway, for the other 5 billion people in the world.

And here I must share with you my interpretation of the story of Jesus, with the little historical facts we know. The incarnation of a savior had been announced and expected for quite some time. He was to be born from a virgin. As it turned out, from a *12-13 year old* girl (child) named Mary. Joseph was her fiancé. Until there, things are half believable. Now is when the sauce starts sticking to the bottom of the pan...

Let's go along with the story of Christians. God sent his begotten son to wash out the sins of human beings who were created with the original sin. Some will tell me, that's not exactly the way it happened and they will proceed, if I let them, to raise the wick of my lamp a few notches, and start to illuminate me with the story of Adam and Eve. They will only start; because, you see, I have been raised catholic and on top of that, I spent ten years in a catholic seminary. Not that I planned to become a priest, but that it was the only way to get a B.A. degree in French Québec, in the fifties. So ten years of room and board and all teachers and guardians *(...jailors)* were catholic priests...

So let's get back to logic. God is omnipotent, omniscient and omni-intelligent. He knows everything that has happened, will happen (up to a point) and will not happen. God in fact doesn't know those things; He is those things. Therefore, God doesn't operate like us! *Wow! Thank God for that!!!*

15

MARY THE VIRGIN...

"Now the birth of Jesus Christ took place in this way. When his mother Mary had been betrothed to Joseph, before they came together she was found to be with child from the Holy Spirit."

Matthew 1:18

Now, I don't want to sound ruthless, Mario Jorge, my brother. This is only my vision of the events. I know we're not supposed to have opinions, different from the church, but having given back my membership card to the Church, *I'm not under its spell anymore...* Here it is.

Mary, who was a virgin, *we're told*, becomes impregnated by the operation of the *Holy Ghost*, without the fertilization of her ovum by a spermatozoid. Before saying that the Mother of God was fooling around with Joseph, I will look at a theory that has been brought up as a possible explanation of *the long distance impregnation...* There's that theory of parthenogenesis that has been flunked around for centuries by some people attempting to make us believe that fairy tale. In 815 A.D., you could sell the theory of parthenogenesis to just about any indoctrinated person, who did or didn't have a clue what it meant.

By the year 1815 AD, the sales had dropped quite a bit. But in 2023 A.D., it hardly sells at all and only to some disorientated lunatics.

"The telescope destroyed the firmament, did away with the heaven of the New Testament, rendered the ascension of our Lord and the assumption of his Mother infinitely absurd, crumbled to chaos the gates and palaces of the New Jerusalem, and in their places gave to man a wilderness of worlds."

Robert G. Ingersoll, Some Mistakes of Moses

I'm no biologist, gynecologist or any kind of "gist", for that matter… I'm also not a chef, but I can cook an omelet better than any chicken I ever met! And, having been raised on a farm, I met a few chicks; the ones with feathers …and others. Here's what I know about parthenogenesis.

It's never been proven that there is a remote possibility that a human being born by parthenogenesis could survive without help from modern biology. And I don't know why they would bother… After all, there are over 3 ½ billion males on the planet who would volunteer for the job of making a baby, without calling any ghost, *holy or not*… We, the male half of the earth's population are known to be very generous when it comes to the recruitment of the troops…

But let us be generous once more and give the fairy tale a chance. Let's pretend we fall for it. Mary was an exception and got pregnant without *"knowing"* a man in the bible sense of the word… So Mary is a virgin and she gives birth to a son they call Jesus. If you look up the etymology of the name Jesus, you find that it *"comes from the Latin form of the Greek name Ἰησοῦς (Iēsous), a rendition of the Hebrew Yeshua (יֵשׁוּעַ), also used as Joshua or Yesua. (63) The name is thus related to the Hebrew consonantal verb, root ysʾ (to rescue or deliver) and the Hebrew noun yešuaʿ (deliverance)."*

Wikipedia

55

For God to have to send His only begotten son on earth to fix the problems so that everybody doesn't have to burn in hell for ever, after they die, it means two things to me. First, either He didn't foresee that men were weak and dumb and that they would screw up. If He is God, which means He's perfect, He could not have been ignorant of what humans are like and what they would or would not do. Otherwise, it means that we can outsmart him… *He is God, not our stupid government, for God sake!* So that first option is impossible.

The second option: He has given free will to humans. If we have free will –and I believe we do– and He interferes to put us back on the right track when we screw up, do we have free will then? If He could come and undo any action we have decided to commit or pick up the broken pieces after the fact, there wouldn't be any final consequences to our actions. So, if it was the case, we would not learn from our mistakes, or we could try anything stupid and if it's going to be catastrophic for mankind, God would interfere to save humanity!

I'm not too familiar with God's agenda, but where was He on August 6th and Aug. 9th 1945? He could have saved between 150,000 and 250,000 human beings in Hiroshima and Nagasaki! Did He screw up? I don't believe so. God has created us and everything else in the creation. He loved us enough to give us free will, in spite of the fact that He knew we would screw up.

But in His infinite wisdom, He also knew that making mistakes is the best, if not the only way for us to learn love and patience. As Edgar Cayce, "the sleeping prophet", reveals to us, Time, Space and Patience explain the essence and the functioning of the creation.

There is no atrocity big enough we could commit that would get God to interfere and change The Law! If we do not do something about what is happening right now to people and to the planet, I'd better be wrong about God not interfering in human affairs!

In *"Coercion: The Achilles Heel of Education"* that I published in Aug. 2014, I maintain "that among the dramatic cultural changes that we should consider seriously, are curbing the warming up of the planet and the overpopulation. If the masses would be made aware of the imminent risks of overpopulation and encouraged to limit their families to no more than two children, we would see a stabilization of the population and even a decrease, possibly. That alone would stop or at least postpone the collapse of civilization. The second threat of an imminent collapse has to do with our "carbon footprint"

"The central challenge, of course, is to phase out more than half of the global use of fossil fuels by 2050 in order to forestall the worst impacts of climate disruption, a challenge the latest International Energy Agency edition of World Energy Outlook makes look more severe."

Paul R. Ehrlich†⇓ and Anne H. Ehrlich

We have the smarts, we have the knowledge, we have the desire; let us take back the power that belongs to us the people and that –till now– we have very irresponsibly let the establishment use to run and exploit us in the most unscrupulous ways.

"There is no nonsense so gross that society will not, at some time, make a doctrine of it and defend it with every weapon of communal stupidity."

Robertson Davies

Mario Jorge, my brother, claiming to be born from a virgin was far from being original for (semi) deities of that era, as we can see by the following document from the web. *"Of the following (semi) deities, legends went around that they were all born of a virgin:*

Augustus (his father was the god Apollo) Agdistis , Attis, Adonis, Buddha, Dionysus, Korybas, Krishna, Mithras, Osirus, Perseus, Remus and Romulus, Tammuzand, Zoroaster and Jesus. Mithras Christianity, Jdstone.org/cr/files/mithraschristianity.html

16

God

"To believe in God or in a guiding force because someone tells you to is the height of stupidity. We are given senses to receive our information within. With our own eyes we see, and with our own skin we feel. With our intelligence, it is intended that we understand. But each person must puzzle it out for himself or herself."

Sophy Burnham

Writing a chapter on God should be a very humbling experience, and more suitable to a Mario Jorge than to a Roméo... On the other hand, if God exist's, He created me. What better references can I give you than I am the son of the almighty God? If He is, and I believe He is, He created me and He is perfect. *How could I be a lemon...?*

One of my sisters often tells me that something **has** to happen! Her reasoning is this one: "the world is going to the dump; God cannot let that happen! Something **has** to happen", meaning : God **has** to interfere! I always have the same answer for her: *"Don't hold your breath, Sister!"*

Right or wrong, Mario Jorge, my brother, … *"Bergoglio!* Are you still with me?" Good! I was saying, right or wrong, I believe that God has thrown the ball (creating the world) in a certain direction, at a certain speed, with a certain upright angle or perfectly level, and He will not come and change the direction of the ball or where it is supposed to land. Why? *Because He is God!* **He doesn't throw foul balls!**

Is it possible that he gave us a tool that we can use to change the direction of the ball and where it's likely to fall, if needed? That tool that we all have and that some …have succeeded in learning how to use is called: *intelligence*. It's more like a tool kit than like a tool. And in that kit, among other things, we find the intelligence. In spite of the appearances to the contrary …in some instances, we all have that tool. I will in the next chapter treat of it more at length.

Coming back to God and what I call his non-interference in the world affairs, I have to try and explain what I mean by that. Can God, being who He is and how He is, about which we know very little other than that He might exist, have given us talents and aptitudes to deal with this "imperfect world," as some call it? Being God, He has to have always existed and will always exist. If he had been created, He would not be God. His creator would be God.

Some will tell me that I don't know anything about God, since I'm an agnostic. By saying that, they insinuate that they know God since He has revealed Himself to them through the revelation that they received through indoctrination from the Church, based on the scriptures, especially the Bible.

I'll use an example to illustrate how I conceive intelligence and God …*maybe*. When you're walking during winter and you arrive at the park, you can sometimes see an imprint/drawing left by a person, usually a child, in the fresh snow. It normally informs you that someone has been there, before you, and has been lying down in the snow and has moved his legs in a kind of open and close motion, and he has also moved his extended arms, his hands touching his thighs first, then

60

moving in a semi-circular motion above the head. It leaves an imprint in the snow we call an angel.

Seeing this, you realize a child has left an angel "drawing" in the snow for fun. And you're probably right. Other than this information, what more can you infer? There's nobody there; only the modified perimeter of a person. I say modified because the movement has left a form different from the one of a person lying down would have left, from his/her shoulders up and from its hips down.

The information left behind is therefore limited. Despite that, the imprint of the angel has left you with some important information. If you estimate the distance from the top of the head to the lower part of the drawing, the feet, you can find the approximate age of the child, with its height, the length of his arms and legs. If the imprint is 3 to 4 feet in height, from head to toes, the child maybe, let's say between 3 and 5 years old. But if the design is from around 5 to 6 feet long from head to toes, the possible range of ages might vary much more. It might be a 15 to 17 years old, or even an adult.

It looks a lot like a normal everyday life's situation. Things are not always simple. Nevertheless, if we look closely at it, we can, most of the time, gather valuable, even crucial information. This is probably the longest detour you've ever seen someone take to talk about God... But I'm coming to the point...

If you think about my example of perimeter in the snow, it's a lot similar. I cannot describe God as such, but I can see through the cracks of my ignorance, some small glimmers of His perimeter. We do not see Him; we see signs of His presence. And I do not pretend knowing Him more than by what I observe in the creation.

I know very little about sculpture, but when I see a beautiful sculpture, I never conclude that it grew from a particular type of rock by itself. Immediately, I marvel at the talent of the sculptor who did it, and I wish I would know him and be able to watch him sculpt. But until I meet him, I only know him by its perimeter or by his useful, fun and artistic output. I can deduce that he has a great sense of shapes in space, of proportions, and a sharper sense of observation than the average person.

And if a sculpture suggests to me the existence of a sculptor, the creation suggests to me ...the existence of a cause, a power source, a motor principle responsible for the creative law that has and continues to create and keep in existence and in constant motion all that exists and that is not caused directly or indirectly by man. I therefore conclude that if there is a creation, there is a creator. However I can't picture that creator as a superman, that people see as an old man sitting somewhere in some imaginary heaven, smoking a joint and laughing at us, *the gang of morons... Ha! Ha!*

No, I cannot describe God to you. I would have loved to...but I've never seen Him other than in flowers, birds, trees, the innocent smile of a child, in the heart of a mother, in a hug, laughters with tears, in the eyes of every sincere and empathic person and in any other act of love.

17

Faith

"That deep emotional conviction of the presence of a superior reasoning power, which is revealed in the incomprehensible universe, forms my idea of God."

Albert Einstein

Amazingly enough, according to catholic people, I don't have *"the Faith!"* I hate to point out to them, that between my attitude towards God and theirs, I believe I have more faith in God than they do. For starters, I don't need any book, any proofs or any written guarantee that I'm safe and saved (whatever that means…) I do not worry about my afterlife. If God exists, He is perfect and He knows me …*and that I hate the heat!* I can't stand to stay in the sun other than under a sun umbrella, and a cold drink! He knows I wouldn't last long in hell…unless they have some kind of air conditioning and lots of Bud light…Ha!Ha!

Knowing that, He wouldn't send me there because I looked at the curves of a beautiful woman, since He made us crazy about the other sex. He can very well be God, but He can't have it both ways! He wanted us to reproduce and he didn't want it to be a chore! He wanted us to experience the highest degree of pleasure on Earth, because pleasure gets us closer to self, to others and to God; pleasure is soul building.

Well, Mario Jorge, my brother, He didn't say it in so many words. He's not as much of a chatterbox as I, but he pretty well designed women's bodies and ours to make sure the earth population doesn't get extinct. And to make sure we don't forget,in our busy life, to oblige, He gave us instincts and passions so we would work on it for the first 50 years of our life, day in day out… with assiduity, enthusiasm and the dedication of *a rabbit on Viagra!*

"Faith: not wanting to know what is true.

Friedrich Nietzsche

I started my life with a load of beliefs in something foreign to me… and to all the others. Of all these beliefs, none were the result of our innate built-in curiosity which motivates us towards self discovery, the discovery of others and of the world around us.

That's the way God, in his infinite wisdom, had drawn the blueprints of the human being I was at birth. We get born perfectly in accordance with our maker's design. And then…education comes and alienates us!

Education at home, education in church, education in school and the socio-cultural education, to name a few… Of all those, real life experiencing is the only one that can't screw you up. All the others can …*and some do.* The worse one is probably the school, given the period of time involved; 12 years of intellectual and mental abuse in most cases! Home education goes from the very good to total disaster. And I'm not pretending that I was among the very good parents! Let's look at the school education …or its lack thereof.

«Believe in yourself, and the rest will fall into place. Have faith in your own abilities, work hard, and there is nothing you cannot accomplish.»

Brad Henry

18

Prayer

"Prayer is not asking. It is a longing of the soul. It is daily admission of one's weakness. It is better in prayer to have a heart without words than words without a heart."

Mahatma Gandhi

There are as many definitions of prayer as there are praying people... But one of them seems to better define the traditional notion of prayer. Here it is:

"Elevation of the soul towards God (or deity) to express to Him one's adoration or veneration, one's thanks or thanksgiving to obtain His graces or His favors; act by which we address the saints to obtain their intercession with God." (Translated from French by the author)

(Monod, Sermons, 1911, p. 207)

That is pretty close to the definition of prayer for Catholics. I certainly not agree with that conception of a conversation/relationship with God. I see it more as an act of begging or bribing people (saints) close to a tyrant, in order to be spared from his anger and his cruelty…

"one's thanks or thanksgiving to obtain His graces or His favors;" sounds more like flattery, plotting and mere prostitution than prayer to me. And this last part takes the cake: *"we address the saints to obtain their intercession with God. (!!!)"* (The exclamation marks are from the author) Mario Jorge, my brother, I know that Monod was a protestant and that it might not be the exact Catholic definition of prayer. But it's certainly close to what the Church taught me prayer was. Should one have to use politics, ruse and plotting to talk to his own father??? If I check my Petit Robert dictionary, I find this for prayer definition: *"Movement of the soul seeking a spiritual communication with God by rising towards Him feelings(recognition, love and adoration)."* (translation…from French by the author).

That is very reasonable and easily acceptable by the majority of people. Much of what Catholics call prayer, like the rosary, repeating again and again formulas learned by heart, has, for me, another name than prayer. I call that pious jargons or drivel, showing a brainwashing and a sad credulity, almost imposed on people *who are not wary enough of the dangers of unbridled indoctrination.*

What should prayer be? I certainly can't answer for others. Prayer is an act that is as personal and delicate as a declaration of love to your life partner, a word of encouragement to a homeless person lying on the sidewalk in the heat …on the harsh concrete. It's roaring with laughter with friends or it is to swoon in front of a flower that is ready to bloom, or watching a hummingbird positioning itself in front of a flower opening, ready to insert its sharp syringe like beak… To pray is also to think about one's brother dying of cancer and to suffer with him, while he's there, powerless, looking death straight in the face without clinching, minute after minute, day after day and hoping he finds the strength to continue to bear this unimaginable burden; *unimaginable until we are there ourselves…*

To pray is to listen to music that transports you to a magical world and coax you to meditate on the miracle of life that has allowed this virtuoso to create a nirvana that takes you back to the childlike candor and innocence and makes us fall in love with life, all over again… To pray is many things to many people including to religious people.

Sometimes people say to you: *"I'll pray for you."* For many people, this gesture is comforting. For me, not quite, and here's why. That a religious somebody tells me that he or she will pray for me, I see this as being very condescending and haughty. They say five little words and you can, if you listen carefully, hear the gears churning in their head. Under their breath, some think something like this:

"You are a poor lost soul who has moved away from the path of truth of which we Catholics have the monopoly. We are saved and you, you're burning" rubber *"on the highway to hell. Obviously, you're not very smart, because otherwise, you'd be Catholic as the intelligent people we are. Please, God, have mercy on this poor erratic creature, half evil, half human"*.

"God is a comedian playing to an audience that is too afraid to laugh."

Voltaire (1694 1778)

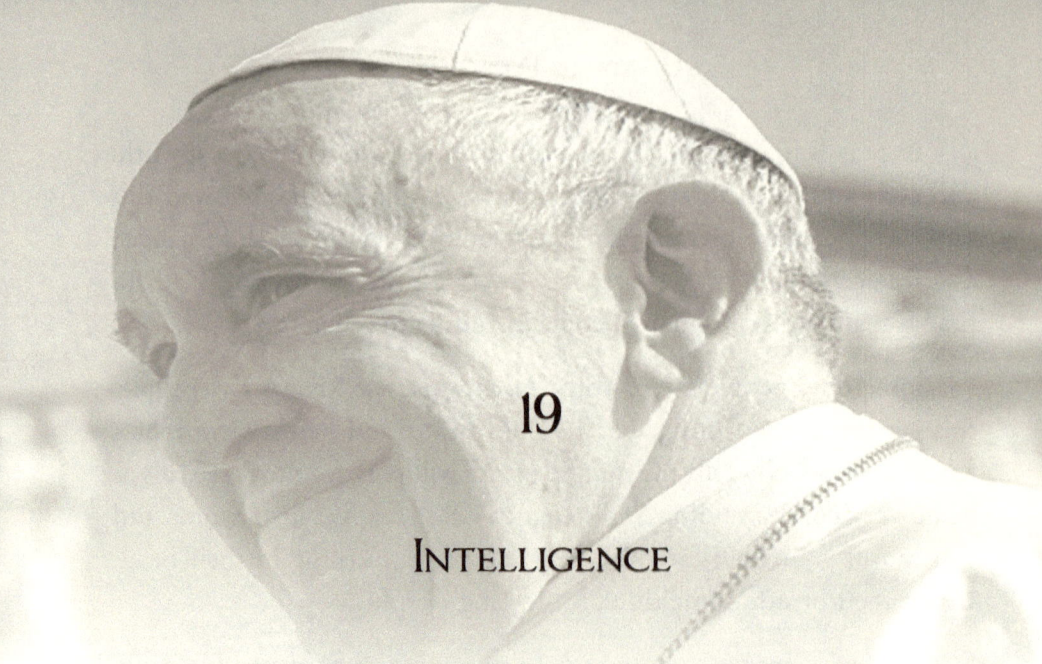

19

INTELLIGENCE

"Beware when the great God lets loose a thinker on this planet.""

Ralph Waldo Emerson (1803 1882)

S ince the early 1900s, we have attempted to measure the intelligence using many types of tests. And the most common of these was called the famous Intelligence Quotient or IQ test. It has been used and abused in an exaggerated way in our schools especially, in spite of its validity being increasingly questioned. We can measure the weight, the height and other body measurements easily. But when it comes to measuring intelligence, it is much less evident.

Mario Jorge, my brother, here's how I see it. God would have given us a tool kit, in which He would have put the intelligence as one of the finest and most essential tool. Most people consider intelligence as the most powerful tool they have ever received. They are proud of their tool, and tend to put it at the top of the list, when they beef up their self-esteem. And we all tend to judge the level of intelligence of people,especially by what is coming out of their mouth when they speak... or of their pen when they write…

There is no doubt that what we say reflects our intelligence *or the use we make of it*. But more and more, we begin to consider the result of our actions more important than our intellectual level in itself. You can have a vehicle with an engine of 300 horsepower, producing less than your neighbor's who has a vehicle with 150 horsepowers but weighing less than half the weight of your car. But let us drop physics to return to… *metaphysics…*

One thing that speaks more of total intelligence than IQ is the emotional quotient or EQ. Instead of only considering the strength of the engine, we measure the output of the traction wheels. We can therefore say that we measure the useful performance of the car —or the positive performance of the person.

Our tool kit, in addition to intelligence might also contain a wide variety of tools allowing us to provide a positive return in the conduct of our lives and that, to varying degrees, depending on a multitude of factors.

Among these factors which are probably not all identified, I include genetic inheritance and archetypes, although their influence is not automatic. Personally, I think we mention them especially when a person turns bad …never when he/she turns ok. I think we often use genetic inheritance to excuse our mistakes or certain unethical conduct we are accused of.

Among other tools in our chest containing intelligence, we have reasoning, judgment, understanding, discernment and sometimes… wisdom etc., which we can develop to different degrees. *We have no merit for being intelligent.* But all these fine tools will only produce positive results if we use the most powerful ingredient in the creation. In fact the creation is completely made of it! What could be that mysterious ingredient that makes us the next best thing after God himself? No, it's not WD 40…or even duct tape! It's a zillion times better, and there is a reserve of it the size of a million universes! Give up??? It's Love!!!

Intelligent love is a gift of life, part of the package deal. We're born with it. We can over the years, learn how to become more skillful in how we use our tool kit, in the same manner as one can learn to use an indented chisel for wood carving. The fact that one owns all the tools of the sculptor does not make him a qualified sculptor. No more than being gifted with a very strong intelligence makes us act intelligently, i.e. lovingly. There's no other way to travel through a happy ever after life. Love is the fuel of our vehicle and it's eco/user friendly… and free! It's God's gift to us. He said so!

Let's consider an example. We hear more and more about people texting while they drive. Most of them work for companies that pay them well for their work, and have been for years. These people have normal or above normal intelligence. However, many believe that it is more dangerous to drive while texting, than to drive with an alcohol level of .08, which is accepted as being impaired.

Many will tell me that those people are stupid. Personally I would say that they are acting very irresponsibly towards other people on the road, including pedestrians. The pleasure of playing on their gadget doesn't seem to warrant the risk to their lives and that of others, including their own children sometimes.

So why do they do it? I do not know the real reason, and I can only assume that they do it to escape the boredom of rush hour driving, of their work and of their lives …maybe! It is a drug like any other drug, at their fingertips and it costs nothing …except fines, sometimes, and damage to vehicles, *when it's not injuries or perfectly preventable deaths.*

And before we throw the stone at that person, we must remember that we are all irresponsible to different degrees. I often say to anyone who will listen, that the *only stupid animal in all of the creation is man.* It is also the wildest and most dangerous!

Let me explain why I chose to write a chapter on intelligence, in a book about the Catholic religion. Before you think I'm inferring that

Catholics are not intelligent, it's absolutely not the case. Catholics are no more no less intelligent than members of any other religion or than agnostics. Belonging to that religion does not speak of the intelligence of the person. According to my beliefs, it can speak of the intrinsic freedom of the person. When we are born into a religion, and that we are indoctrinated into that religion by our parents, by the church and often by the culture, including school, we are not intellectually free people. We are indoctrinated people, conditioned people and have been victims of a strong brainwashing like I have been and most of the world has been. These people are as intelligent as you or me, but are not free to think what they think and believe what they believe. They were violated intellectually, mentally and spiritually, and continue to be abused by a system of beliefs that uses seduction, (promise of eternal happiness) and coercion, (threat of hell) to attract and keep people in line.

ASK THE DOVE . . .

One day, curious, I asked the beautiful white dove,

The coveted secret from cradle to the grave,

That impregnates your life, with an eternal love,

And that gives its color for you to love and crave.

The discreet charming dove cooed very tenderly,

Arranged her plumage, flattered by my request: "

Answer to the enigma haunting you constantly,

Can't be found in science nor in scientist's quest!

Go question the swallow, the sparrow, the blue jay,

Where they get energy, their good mood, their singing?

Get down low, if you please, look at the rose, you may.

Its grace and its color, and its divine smelling.

To the kitten, the cub, the entire nature,

What is the ingredient of their great alertness,

Mystery that haunts you, and intrigues and tortures.

The dolphin, the otter, their plays, their foolishness,

And all, in their language, their murmur, their twitter,

Their wing flaps, their soaring, you must believe me, Man,

Will give you a drawing, an image, a picture,

Made of plants and of birds, animals and humans.

Put your hands in the earth, from inside from outside,

Your head up in the clouds, your face in the flowers,

Renew your connection with the cosmos, don't hide,

Re-attach missing link; give the heart its power!

Then you will understand, not with your head alone,

Like those pseudo scholars, but from inside your heart,

Like children always do, in more ways than one,

Cause Love is everywhere, for all on this good Earth!"

Demande à la colombe, Roméo Gauvreau, Jan.2000,

Ask the dove

English translation May 2013

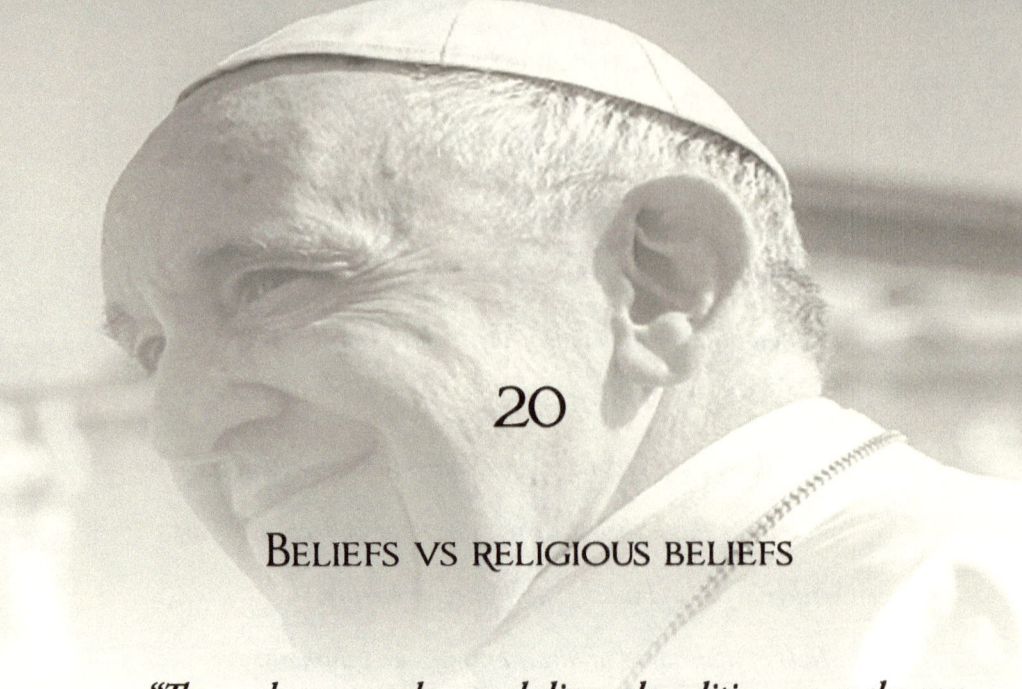

20

BELIEFS VS RELIGIOUS BELIEFS

"Those who can make you believe absurdities can make you commit atrocities."

Voltaire (1694 1778)

I would like to juggle a bit with three concepts that come up in our conversations: beliefs, knowledge and know how (skills). We start very young to know certain things, such as pain or discomfort caused by a wet diaper. Pretty soon, we learn that crying draws attention to us, and when mother is alerted, the diaper very often gets replaced or we receive some food mixed with warmth and loving touch. Therefore crying is a way of getting certain needs satisfied.

Can we therefore say that the baby already has some knowledge or expertise? Knowledge, for me, is only the storage of information. We do not necessarily understand the things we know. I know the formula of the law of Eienstein's relativity, E = MC2. But I do not understand it. We all know what a TV is, but we don't really know how it brings pictures from Titicaca to our living room in Canada or anywhere else on earth.

When we talk about the pain caused by a hammer hit on a thumb, even if it has never happened to us, we have the information that it hurts. But, after the fact, we *know* that it hurts and how much it hurts, because we have experienced it at the sensations level, and not only at the intellect level. It is a life experience; it's knowledge/knowhow or *experience*.

When I was young, I believed in hell like if it was real. God instructed people had driven it in my head with threats. It was indoctrination. I had to deny myself, not to listen to my doubts, and make myself believe notions, I often did not believe. They had told me that I had to believe it just the same because it was a mystery. I had to make an act of faith or ... *make myself believe that I believed ... even if I didn't*.

The Church was forbidding me to use my judgment and my conscience. They were telling me that I had to bypass my conscience and make an act of faith and believe what I found non believable! It was intellectual dishonesty, mental masturbation and spiritual prostitution, ...in the name of God!

In reality, Mario Jorge, my brother, what they were asking from me was to make an act of faith in a man, *that priest*, and not an act of faith in God. God hasn't asked me to make an act of faith in Him, in the last 85 years!

The Catholic Church had asked me to do that for the first 25 years of my life, until I woke up and told it where to go! And, in my opinion, one of the best things I've ever done for my children was to not raise them in *any* religion, or to impose *"a", "or my god"*. on them. If there is one, I trust them/Him that they will find Him/Her, *if they choose to!* It is not up to me to decide *whom* they shall love, *human or divine!*

What would you think if I told you: the heavens opened up, last night, and explosions of thunder and great light, and a vessel shining like metal descended and landed on earth and the pilot (the Lord) came out of it and talked to me. He gave me an Ipad (scroll, table of law???)

on which his instructions were written (the will of the Lord and of his Father from a distant galaxy where everything is better than here : heaven!

"A savior will come and inform you about the change to bring about,(teach the Gospel) to turn the ship around and repair your mistakes (your sins). He wants to save you (He loves you) and will provide the necessary technology and even pay for the cost, even if it kills him (being very generous, giving his life in some way).

All you have to do to be spared from what is to be expected because of the initial errors of greedy corporations (original sin coaxed on men by those devils) is to trust my father (have faith in God), and you will be spared from this devilish heat, (global warming, hell) that will be the end of life on earth!

If you do what I'm telling you, you will be saved (you will go to heaven) and the earth will be saved (from hell). Verily, I say unto you: correct your mistakes (repent), stop using fossil fuels (cease sinning against nature) and commit these crimes (sins) against the cosmos (God). You are on earth in 2023, and unless you follow my instructions to the letter, you will end up like in "a fiery furnace" (global warming) where you'll burn for not heeding to (disobeying me) this warning! "

Where am I going with this strange gibberish, Mario Jorge, my brother? In the last four paragraphs, I presented a description of a fictional encounter between an earthling and a messenger from a distant planet inhabited by a civilization that is much more advanced than ours, technically and hopefully, socially. For some reason, that civilization does not want us to destroy the earth.

Perhaps it's because the earth is very rich in some mineral, non-existing on their planet. They use these minerals in large quantities in their technology and medicine and in some components used in some technology comparable to our computer technology, but much more advanced. Their technology is a distant ancestor of our technology.

It's a lot like what we call the philosopher's stone, but boosted to an extent that no one would believe its capabilities. It is said that the famous philosopher's stone could change ordinary metals, into precious metals, such as creating gold or silver from lead, for example, cure diseases or even prolong human life beyond what we would dare hope for!

I shared with you my beliefs of a possible explanation of the birth of the Catholic religion. What would you think if I went to visit a primitive tribe and tell them the same story I just told you, and I would tell them that it is the Truth revealed by God, and that they do not have the choice to believe or not to believe it ... under the threat of death! (...inquisition ?)

And I would leave some of my associates behind with the tribe to report to me and reassure me that they're complying with my "doctrines", while they, (my partners) abuse adults with tyrannical teachings, especially women, and rape some of their young boys and girls in a very perverse way. They would have to endure these sexual abuses knowing that the outside world must not find out about it, because I'm well connected and my men *cannot be brought to justice ... as it has been the case with the Catholic Church's sexual abuses by priests for the last 50 years???*

Wouldn't that be an abominable crime punishable by a long prison term? Wouldn't the United Nations intervene quickly to the defense of these poor peoples. And wouldn't the courts parade us, me and my associates, in the news worldwide, to show everyone how such vile acts of cunning and hypocrisy, under the banner of holiness deserve to be punished harshly???

Is there a slight possibility that what they called the Lord was an ET who came to earth, as they have done many times before and continue to do so regularly to this day? And that, for reasons that our governments know but don't want us to know? They believe that they are gods and they look down on us as on cockroaches that ought not to be squashed ...as long as we pay our dues. and say please and thank you...

The whole content of this indoctrination, if we accepted it as truth, constituted our religious beliefs. We were told – and believed– that thinking about a woman sexually, was a mortal sin that we had to confess to the priest, if we didn't want to spend eternity in hell! Between you and me, my brother, if you are heterosexual and most of us are, do we have the choice never to think about a woman sexually? We have the choice to *try* to stop to think about her in that manner... My first question is: why would we? And my second question is: is it possible that the Church is *out to lunch* on that one?

The sexual drive is a perfectly normal, healthy and beneficial attraction towards the opposite sex, a very important instinct given to man/woman by God to assure the survival of the species, which instinct, I believe, is stronger than the instinct for survival of the individual.

And concerning our religious beliefs, *Mario Jorge*, my brother, our parents, *who knew everything,* supported the "men of the cloth" 100%. Who were we to doubt their teachings? So we held these things as the truth. Now I no longer believe in the Catholic Church teachings. These are my new beliefs. But I can't prove they were wrong. And I can't prove that I'm right to believe what I believe now. *I think* they were wrong and *I think* I'm right not to believe them anymore. So beliefs and knowledge do not necessarily imply the truth.

"I never cease being dumbfounded by the unbelievable things people believe.."

Rosten (1908-1997)

When I hear on TV that Islamabad is the capital of Pakistan, I have just received a unit of information. It's now part of my beliefs. Do I know that Islamabad is the capital of Pakistan? Is it part of my knowledge? I have no proof that this is true. If and when I go to Pakistan, and visit the capital, if it's Islamabad, then I will know for sure. Meanwhile, I believe that it's true. Our beliefs are probably true 10% of the time and wrong 90% of the time.

Therefore, what are beliefs? How are they useful to us if most of the time they are scientifically false? I will make a distinction between beliefs, things that we believe, and religious beliefs: things we have been told *we had to believe!* In this case, I am talking about regular beliefs, things that we believe. We all sail on the sea of life with a head full of data. This is the content of our hard drive on our "computer" (brains).

Now, like on the hard drive of our computer or memory, there are millions of units of information. This is the content of our memory, our knowledge, our beliefs, our know-how: our intellectual baggage and all our life experiences. If we became neurotic and decided we would only believe what we have proofs of, or what is scientifically proven, we would cease to function. Because the amount of scientifically proven things, compared with the total of available information is like a drop of water compared to a full bath of water!

It has been preached to us for centuries that cow's milk was a staple of nutrition. How many people believe it now? Not wanting to be sued by the Department of agriculture, I will only say that my last glass of milk dates back to 1950. For centuries, wheat bread was considered like the mainstay of nutrition. It's about the same story with white bread. If they did not add vitamins to it, I've been told, they would have to sell it with the junk food; not as a real food.

The remarks I made to my students one day, about knowledge, might sound strange to you. But I truly believed what I told them and that I reproduce here for you:

"If I tell you that I'm more than you with the arrogant attitude of the one who knows everything, in the same breath, I'm telling you that you are less than me, and that, I know that it's wrong! True knowledge, starts when one really knows that we know nothing. The true knowledge is to be fully oneself! When we accept that "We must free ourselves from the

known", ("Se libérer du connu") as Krishnamurti's book tells us to, allows us to really accede to the true knowledge, the nirvana of Buddhism. With that liberation, you will know "how" instead of "what"! That's, in brief, what I think when I look at you."

In summary, we have knowledge that we think we know and our beliefs are most of the time vital and can sometimes be fatal. To demonstrate my point of view saying that our beliefs influence our lives in a way greater than we might believe, I will relate an incident that I read about in an article whose source I do not remember. But I remember the story very well.

This is a story about what happened to a young medical student who was hitchhiking to get to his destination. He decided to *"bum a ride"* on the railroad. He jumped into a wagon going in the desired direction, with his "pack sack." He closed the door of the wagon and lit up a candle to write in his diary.

That's when he notices, spelled out on the end wall: *Refrigerated wagon.* He gets up, picks up his "pack sack", go to open the door to jump off the wagon; the door has locked itself from the outside. *He is therefore trapped in this walk-in refrigerator.* He panicks! What will happen to him?

He begins to calculate how many hours he has to spend in this critical situation, before the train arrives at its destination and he gets to be freed. Can he survive the duration of the scheduled railroad trip? He worries with good reasons; he feels increasingly cold. He writes in his diary how he feels as the hours pass. Stiffness is invading his limbs; death is whirling above his head like a buzzard. He's going to fall asleep, he knows, and never to wake up!

He was found dead the next day or the day after, with the written story of the progression of his death, victim of the cold. He had indeed died from the cold. However, I must add that there was no produce in the wagon needing to be kept cold; consequently, *the refrigerating system was not activated.*

Mario Jorge, my brother, *his belief* that he would die frozen had killed him …not the temperature of the wagon, which was well above freezing temperature. Some will tell me that it's part of the law of attraction. It is a theory that I'm aware of, for having read *"Ask and it is given."* Do I believe in it? Somewhat, but not in a religious way. Could it help to ask if you want to receive? Yes, if we ask the right way, for the right reason and to the right source! Do we receive what we ask for? Personally, I don't think so. I think that what it means, essentially, is that it helps to visualize the important things we need for our spiritual life, for our soul journey.

If on a beautiful summer day, I ask for a sunny day to harvest the hay and put it in the barn, and my neighbors pray for rain to grow their tomatoes, "somebody will be disappointed!" I do not believe that prayer force the hand of God and makes Him move in one direction or another. We can *–and do–* manipulate people; I strongly believe we can't manipulate God. Praying God for *favors*, for me, demonstrates a misunderstanding of God and of the soul journey through eternity.

In my conception of a god, I do not believe that God exists as a separate entity from us, separated from our souls. I believe in prayer, but not in drivel, or pious jargons. I see prayer as the formulation of an intention expressed to ourselves, to our soul, an intention to receive the things that we *need* to see materialize in our lives. Prayer remains for me a process of relation to the collective consciousness or the cosmos i.e. God.

I believe, Mario Jorge, my brother, that everything we need, *really need*, for the journey of the soul, the cosmos will be happy to give it to us, if first, we help ourselves. With regard to praying for material gain, like winning the lottery, I find it ridiculous and childish, to say the least!

This detour, I hope, will help to understand more deeply my understanding of what life's journey is about and how we have to face life on our own without the crutch of religious indoctrination.

We all have to find self first, actualize self, get to know self, *the beginning of all knowledge,* and to finally reach love of self, love of others and of God. Then and only then, real life starts. We should not start a family and have kids before we reach that super important point in our life. If we would wait before having kids to reach that threshold, we would act in a more responsible way towards these kids who, otherwise, will have a hard time to reach self-actualization and self-love.

21

SALE OF SEATS IN HEAVEN...

"Heaven goes by favor. If it went by merit, you would stay out and your dog would go in."

Mark Twain

In 1973, a year after moving to British Columbia, I had the opportunity to meet a man from my Gaspé hometown. He had just arrived in B.C. a few months earlier. While chatting about one thing or another, one day, he mentioned his trip to Europe and especially to Rome. Not too many people in the sixties had ever flown in an airplane. Rome was at the other end of the world for us.

So, I was listening with wide open eyes, when he told me with great pride that he had bought indulgences at the Vatican. He added, even bragging about it, that he had paid $1,000.00! He was convinced (but not convincing) that he had just ...secured a seat in heaven for himself! In 1960, $1,000.00 was worth at least 20 times that amount at today's money value! And he thought he knew everything! *A $10 bottle of Scotch or a joint (pot) would have put him in Heaven just the same...Ha! Ha!*

But he was not the only gullible one to get screwed this way. Even today, millions of people around the world pay to have a mass celebrated for all sorts of reasons, but in fact for one and only one reason: to try to buy the favors of God for themselves or others. In politics, it's called contribution to the electoral fund, hoping for favors in return. We all know the expression that says literally: "To grease someone's paw." So "they grease God's paw," hoping for favors in return. How noble!

"Millions of masses are annually celebrated by priests against retribution for individuals. Only the rich can afford the hope of going to Heaven, whatever happens. Some priests live in luxury, sell to others the right to say these masses, and not even set foot in their parishes."

Wikipédia

To those who tell me to be careful with what I read on the internet, Mario Jorge, my brother, I can assure you that I'm very cautious with regard to the sources of the information that bombards us constantly. I watch news on TV with a lot of skepticism. Political, military and religious propaganda is often added to the news.

Do I believe the news on TV? First, I only watch very little news. If for example, I'm not ready to give money or go to Africa and help children who are starving to death, why would I feed my psyche those horrible pictures? I paid for 6 or 7 years to support a small child so that he got fed, clothed and went to school. And that, until one day someone told me to research how my money was used to "help small Africans a little ...*and big capitalists a lot!*" There would be volumes to write about the exploitation *"of us poor suckers"*

I'll just say this: when I learn that some CEOS at the head of such organizations are up to one million three hundred thousand dollars a year in salary, plus expenses accounts of hundreds of thousands of dollars, with luxurious homes and luxury cars provided, plus paid vacations for them and their family, several times a year, etc., I take my little mirror, I look at myself and I say: *"You stupid sucker!"*

The day when, Mario Jorge, my brother, instead of keeping feeding starving children, with another child arriving every year or so, we will provide mothers of these children with the birth control devices, and explain to them that they are prolonging death instead of saving lives, it might help solve the problem! The problem is a cultural problem first, including cultural indoctrination and, too often, religious indoctrination. If Africa would get rid of archaic religion teachings and help to educate the masses and encourage them to use birth control, eventually it would reduce hunger and the unnecessary sufferings it causes.

I think it is criminal to continue to give birth to children, we know very well, will die of hunger in large numbers. If culture and some religions would stop cramming their heads (African women's) and tell them that it is God's will that they have as many children as they can and that God will provide for these children(…it's not happening), it would save lots of sufferings. These women gradually would get a hold of their senses, their maternal and nurturing nature and would realize that they are the cause of a horrific infanticide.

The Catholic Church has been selling indulgences for over 1500 years. It supposedly means the total or partial remission of sins. Such dubious business seems like a hoax to me! Giving indulgences for a monetary gift can be said in a different way. It's simpler and more honest to say: "We (the Church) are selling seats in Heaven..." I heard that they have paid for the construction of the Vatican with the revenues of *indulgence peddling* and could be largely financing its operation the same way in 2023! But they didn't open their books for me to see...

The Catholic Church, Mario Jorge my brother, is an ''ambitious and proud business." It has a gargantuan and psychopathic thirst for power. It is run by people who have been indoctrinated and who have been brainwashed with *''mawkish'' religiosity,* that only people who have been subjugated and brainwashed by a systematic indoctrination can accept.

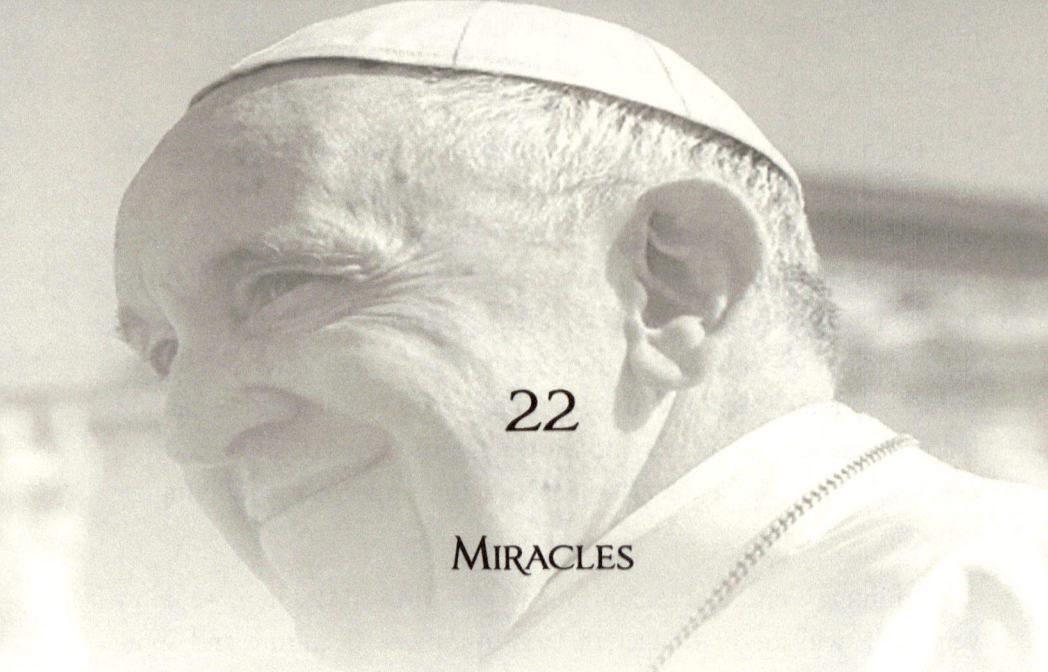

22

MIRACLES

"In a secular age, an authentic miracle must purport to be a hoax, in order to gain credit in the world."

Angela Carter

Like almost everyone, from a very young age, I've heard of miracles. The kind of miracles I heard about were, of course, religious miracles. Those, according to the Catholic religion, are the result of a direct intervention of god.

Some of the best known, for Catholics at least, are the miracles of the apparitions at Fatima and Lourdes. There were also the miracles of Brother André in Montreal who would have cured thousands of people. And you all know other cases of miracles, especially healing miracles. I must bring a distinction here between the miracles of Fatima and the miracles of Brother André. This last one, as far as I know, was healing people by his psychic powers and not by god's direct intervention.

One of the best known healers in the world was Edgar Cayce, known as "the sleeping prophet." He has been followed and extensively scrutinized for his psychic healing powers.

Closer to us, Mario Jorge my brother, there's John of God in Brazil who is seeing up to 1000 people a day, 3 days a week, and who heals a very high percentage of them. He practices surgery on people who are standing, are conscious and don't show any signs of pain or discomfort. You can watch many videos of him doing surgery, and see if you think it's a hoax! He has been investigated by the media and by surgeons who don't understand how he can perform all these surgeries without gloves ...and without any case of infection, *ever!* And you know what is the real kicker of the story? He charges nothing, zilch, nada ...never! He channels over 30 entities "in the spirit," in the process of healing people.

Don't take me wrong! I believe in miracles. I see them every day in the garden. The seeds my wife buries in the ground go through a transformation process, they find the elements they need for that transformation in the ground and in the water; green plants grow, buds appear and flowers open. Bees pollinate these flowers and some of them become raspberries, blueberries, while others give us delicious tomatoes or cucumbers. Later in the season we enjoy eating our Concord and Champagne grapes. And every day, I eat some of these fruits and vegetables and they become a part of me and operate cellular changes in me, of which we are only beginning to understand the complexity and the beauty.

And every time I see a pregnant woman or a child, Bergoglio my brother, I remind myself that this is the greatest miracle of life! And I'm in awe; my soul smiles! Those who need the Vatican to be convinced of imaginary miracles would simply have to remove the blindfold of indoctrination that made them blind to the real miracles of life, in the first place, to be aware of the multitude of miracles that always abound everywhere around them.

Suppose I'm given a choice between two peoples to educate my child. The first one would be a very religious person who would speak to him/her about the supposed miracles of the alleged apparitions of

Fatima and about some miraculous cures attributed to saints, and would teach him/her prayers that please God etc.

The second would be an agnostic who would be very interested in flowers, birds, insects and would swoon when seeing a butterfly twirling in front of them or a pair of *"lovers who smooch on public benches not caring about the glances of honest passers-by... "*(Georges Brassens)

If one accepts the premise of our hypothesis that these two peoples are equally full of love for children, you can probably guess that my choice would be the agnostic person. What I would reproach the religious person is to indoctrinate my child with unrealities that teach my child intellectual dishonesty. For me, any and all indoctrination from parents, from school, from church or from the media is a crime against human rights.

If you want your child to have a chance at life, keep his/her mind virgin and trust him/her that with his natural innate curiosity he will learn how to read the book of life. Facilitate your kids access to knowledge, but don't decide for them what they should be curious about. Have faith in yourself and in them and they shall find who they are and who the other is. If they reach the "knowti teauton" of (the wise Greeks), or the "know thyself" in modern day language, they will graduate to ''love of self and of others''. Having reached this ultimate level of advancement, you will consequently: ***"Do unto others like you would like them do unto you. "***

This is true religion without indoctrination. This is the utmost example of the miracle of soul evolution or travel for those who believe in the journey of the souls through multiple incarnations in the density ...or in reincarnation.

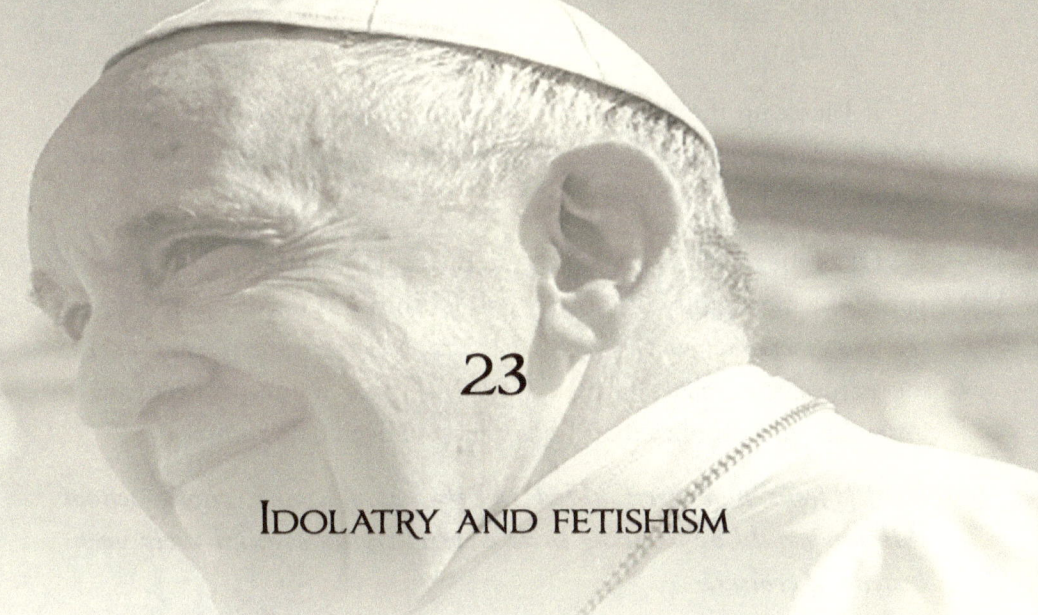

23

IDOLATRY AND FETISHISM

"You shall have no other gods before me. "You shall not make for yourself "a carved image", or any likeness of anything that is in heaven above, or that is in the earth beneath, or that is in the water under the earth. You shall not bow down to them or serve them, for I the Lord your God am a jealous God,..."

Exodus 20:3-6 ESV / 317

What part of "a carved image" does the Catholic Church seems not to understand, Mario Jorge my brother? Carved images...statues of Jesus ...or of the Virgin Mary ... medals ...the cross etc.? Then there are the real pagan rituals like the sprinkling of people with Holy (?) water? And what about the ridiculous censer spewing smoke around the altar or in processions when the priest swings that amulet around like if it had any religious value or magic powers!!! Aren't those all pagan paraphernalia borrowed from previous religions like the Mithraic religion, maybe? Either your bible is wrong ...or you're the leader of a Church perpetrating idolatry! And you say that the Bible is the word of God ??? So, would it be that the Catholic Church goes against its own teachings and sins by pride, "*thinking itself above God*"?

If I look up the definition of idol on the web, I get this: *"Icon or representation of a god, image, effigy, statue, figure, figurine, fetish, totem."*

Of all the religions I heard about, the Catholic religion comes across as the one most guilty of idolatry and fetishism. It seems to me like *the real god of your religion is not God; …it's the Virgin Mary!* The medals, the statues, the images of the Virgin Mary and the rosary seem more important to Catholics than Jesus Christ or even God himself!

"If Jesus had been killed twenty years ago, Catholic school children would be wearing little electric chairs around their necks instead of crosses.

Lenny Bruce

"The exorcists use it thinking that it will scare the devil which they pretend is in the person to be exorcised. There is the way of the cross, The Holy cross, cross on the steeple of every church, everywhere you turn in the church, at the cemetery entrance, on the tombstones, on the school walls, in Catholics' houses, on the beginning of the rosary, around people's neck and on all your garb! "this is pure fetishism, not religion!" People cross themselves; the priest makes the sign of the cross in the air during mass, on the forehead of baby's at baptism, at confession when he pretends to absolve your sins and …ad nauseam"!

What really gets me going is your insistence on the virginity of Mary. The bible treats women *like pieces of dirt* and your Church makes the virginity of Mary a dogma that we must believe without questioning it. Why is it so important for your Church to not only treat women as second class citizens but to subjugate them in a shameful way? You go as far as insinuating that it was not respectful for Jesus to get born as the result of a sexual intercourse. Didn't He choose that method of incarnation for His own mother's birth??? Did He disrespect her in doing so?

90

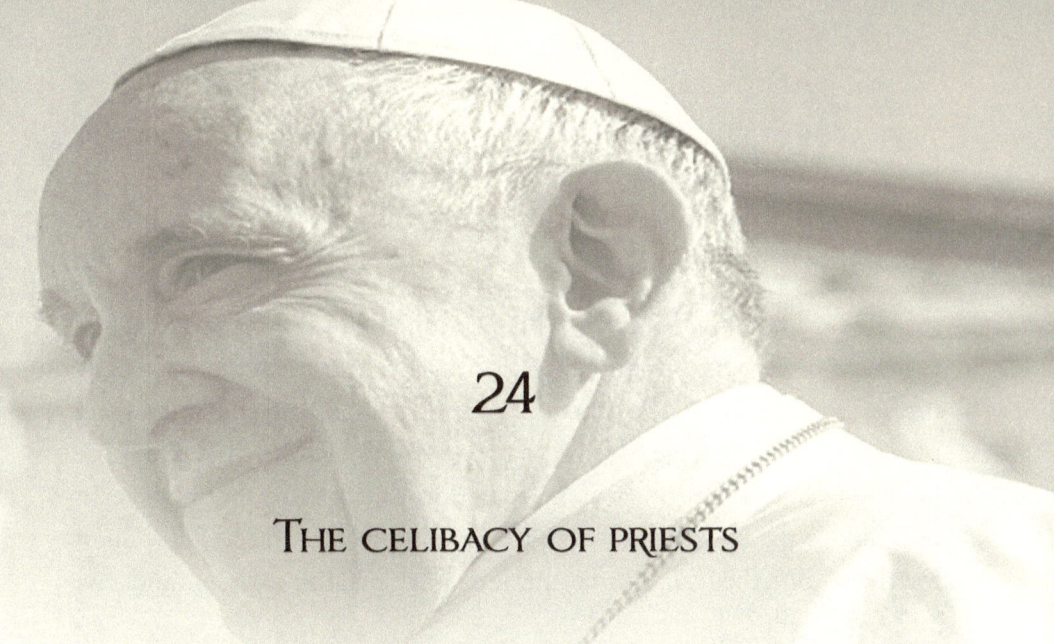

24

THE CELIBACY OF PRIESTS

"Everyone agrees the celibacy rule is just a Church law dating from the 11th century, not a divine command."

Hans Küng

Mario Jorge my brother, what's up with that story about the celibacy of priests? *Why wouldn't they suffer like all of us? Ha!Ha!* Personally, I find it strange and I do not accept their explanations that it's to devote themselves entirely to the service of God. It is a choice against nature which demonstrates to me a misogynist and biased attitude towards women. Going back in time, in the history of the Catholic Church, we realize that there has been a lot of dissension about this questionable policy.

Although my PhD is in *"B.S."* ...and not biology, I firmly believe that being sexual or asexual is not an option as the air conditioning on a car.... This is not something that we have the choice to say: I choose to be a sexual being or an asexual being for the rest of my life. Anybody can go against nature. But there are consequences to suffer and a price to pay...sometimes even by others (abused children)!!! Isn't going against nature to believe oneself smarter than God or to plainly and simply be confused (psycho)? I think it is against nature to decide, for reasons bordering on delusion or religiosity, to override our strongest instinct, the instinct of reproduction for the conservation of the species and for our own spiritual evolution.

This is not something that the government or the Church has the power to dictate to human beings. Nature, the cosmos, the causal law of the universe or God,for most peoples, decided. And if a small gang of...enlightened people, decide that, for wacky reasons, they are more knowledgeable than God in the direction that nature should take in response to the hysteria in which they choose to embark, well! ...Good for them! But they can't force that on other peoples (priests) and say: "It's God's will!"

You can't blame the people from early centuries for being primitive and naive to excess. Their culture had conditioned them to believe that everything that came down from the sky was God himself or his angels. If we thought the same way today, there would be a whole lot of gods and angels in Los Angeles ...and everywhere else where there are airports!

One is not guilty for having been born and being raised dumb, but eventually, we have the right to look at the creation, see the order and intelligence that has set it in place and the laws that govern it. The truth is not in books, but in the great book: I don't mean the bible...but the Book of Life. And that book, we all know how to read it if we accept not to lie to ourselves, for whoever: priest, king, pope or false god! They(the priests) were brainwashed with religious propaganda instilled in them from a very young age. The goal was that they would accept to become fathers/priests instead of fathers/parents and renounce to a normal " *homo sapiens* " life. And when they answer that it's a greater vocation than raising a family, what do they know about the unsurpassed vocation of parent? Where did they get their empirical knowledge and their real life experience? You say that God is perfect, and you concoct a story showing that getting born the way He chose for all of us is not good enough for His son???

And another insult to women: priests are forbidden to get married under the pretense that it would distract from their work as priests. Is it the real honest reason, or is it rather because she is the cause of our perdition, and might not even have a soul...? So, what is the real reason, then, why a woman is not worthy of marrying a priest or becoming priest herself??? *"Did God tell the Church that she was not good enough to belong to the phallocratic elite of your Church? Would God be a Golf sympathizer? Remember the signification of the acronym: G.O.L.F.? "Gentlemen Only Ladies Forbidden?"*

Maybe it would be beneficial to you "all good catholics" and to the world if you put your bible aside for a moment and smell the coffee before peoples realize even more that you are disconnected from reality, from them ...*and maybe from God!* And while you're at it, please try to come back to earth with the rest of the world, like you, Mario Jorge my brother are doing and be our siblings instead of our pretentious fathers! Don't kid yourself; you're nobody's fathers ...*not that we know, anyway!*

Finally, think about my honest advice: get your head out of the clouds ...or of the fairy tales book!

As regards the individual nature, woman is defective and misbegotten, for the active power of the male seed tends to the production of a perfect likeness in the masculine sex; while the production of a woman comes from defect in the active power.

Thomas Aquinas

What an ignorant, biased and misogynistic lunatic!!! Why hasn't the Church, realizing the misogynistic philosophy of that man, reverse its decision and declare him insane ...instead of saint? Of course, he had the approval and the support of the Church and seemingly still has it to this day...

Request to the Curia Romana (not including you, Pope Francis):

"Please apologize to women about the canonization of such a misogynistic, lunatic and uncanonize him, out of respect for women. Think before you declare somebody a saint! Canonizing John XXIII was a great mistake. It might come back to bite your bum and it might not take long either… To force bishops of the world to cover up pedophiles and their crimes is extremely serious. I really don't understand why you canonized him???"

I guess we're all human, even you guys. Take a small step in the direction of recognizing women as human beings with a soul from God …like *most* human beings! Your mother was a woman and she never was as mean to you as you are to her …in 2023 by not repairing your mistakes! Honor her as she deserves to be. It's your mother, *for God's sakes!!!* I admire women for their fortitude and their magnanimity and their incredible self-control for not having blown up your head office…

Another barbarian and misogynistic platitude: **"Sin began with a woman and because of her we all must die."** Ecclesiasticus 25:19,24

"Please, Mario Jorge my brother, just tell your mother, if she's still alive, or tell your sister about that verse. Look her in the eyes and tell her that it's the word of God! And if it's not, as the highest ranked being on earth after God, what are you waiting to remove from the bible that and numerous other terrible and stupid slanders against all women in the world???"

I know your job will not be an easy one! But if you can't stand the heat, Mario Jorge my brother, you should get out of the kitchen! Otherwise, you'd better get cooking; we're hungry …for justice!!!

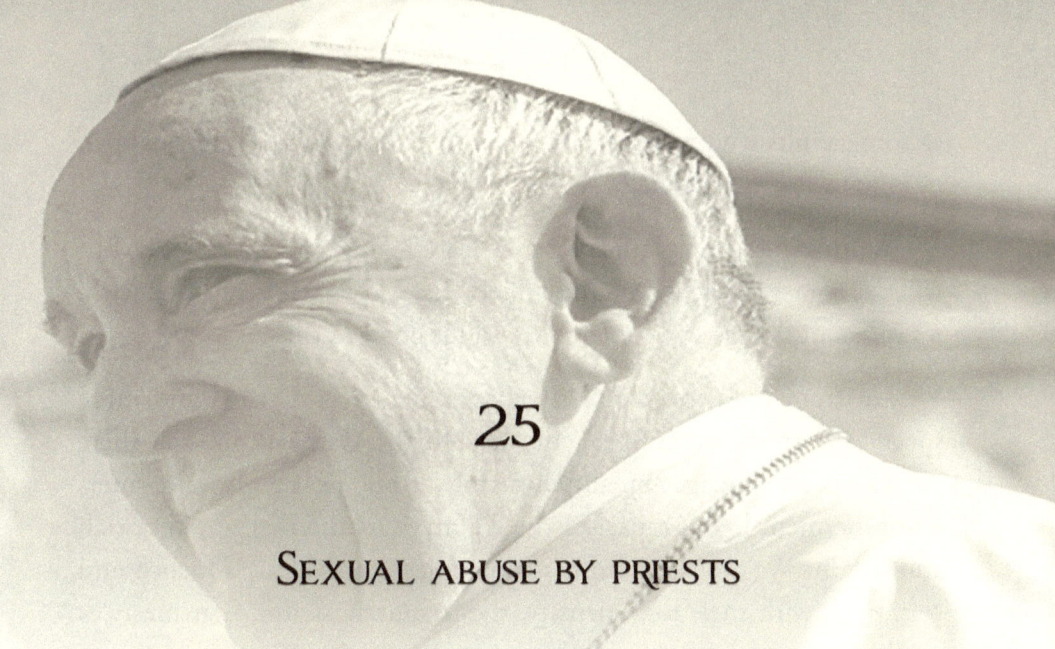

25

SEXUAL ABUSE BY PRIESTS

"If Catholic priests are abusing children, it is Rome, not Dublin, that must answer for it with a full confession and a criminal investigation. Until it does, 'All good catholics, should avoid Mass!" In Ireland, it is time we separated our God from our religion, and our faith from its alleged leaders."

Mike Whitney Global Research

All good catholics should avoid Mass!" And I would add: all kids between the age of 3 and 16, should avoid telling the priest in the confessional that they are sexually active... There's at least a 10% chance they might be talking to a pedophile.... Don't give him ammunitions that might help him *build a trap to get you in his net of deception.* No, I'm not delusional; Mario Jorge my brother, it's not only me... I hear a crescendo of roaring from many corners of society and even from the catholic community. There's a malaise the Church can't manage to ignore or cover up anymore. During the last ten years, we have heard a lot about sexual abuses by priests. There has been several lawsuits and huge sums were paid by the Vatican to parents of abused children and to some adults who were abused when they were young. And I happen to know a few …personally.

Writing for me, is quite easy, at least in my mother tongue. But when it comes to writing on the subject that I'm proposing to deal with, it's different. I feel very vulnerable and for good reasons.

I'm from the province of Quebec, a region of Canada and more specifically from the Gaspé Péninsula. In the Gaspé Péninsula, there were maybe 75 villages inhabited mainly, if not exclusively, by farmers and fishermen. It was a part of the country's nature that was very rich and virgin. We were far from major cities, particularly Quebec and Montreal, with their high density, the trepidations and their lifestyles partly disconnected from nature.

But let's go back in time, 70-75 yrs ago. When we were young, around 12 to14 years old, we had to walk to Church every day for the whole month of May, if my memory is good. We had to walk 2 miles in the morning, and 2 miles after 4 pm to come back home … rain or shine. We had to spend the whole day sitting in silence in the church and listen to catechism or instruction of Catholic doctrines. In modern language, I call that systematic indoctrination or in other words: brainwashing.

All that fla fla, was to prepare us for solemn communion. If you are Catholic, you know too well what it means, and if you're not Catholic, …you don't really want to know!

My younger sister was 13 years old, when she walked to catechism with an older sister. At the end of one of these days, it came to her older sister's ears that the priest had been kind of groping my young sister's burgeoning breasts. My older sister, on her returning home, told my mother what had happened. My mom got mad and scolded my snitching sister for lying and saying bad things about a priest: "Priests can't and don't do that kind of things!"

Guess again, Mom!!! Yes they can, and oh! Yeah! They do!

I must add that this anecdote coming from my family is hearsay only. I wasn't there, but I believe it to be true. Let's forward to about 5 years later. It's now 1951-52.

I was thirteen years old at the time. Having caught the flu or something of that nature, I was in bed in the seminary's infirmary. Here I must open a parenthesis. Each year, the Direction of the Seminary would choose a priest, *any priest*, and make him the students' "doctor" for that year. No knowledge of pharmacy, no knowledge of biology or anatomy or first aid, or even knowledge of CPR: *no problemo!*

Of course nobody called him a doctor. He was the male nurse. He was very calm, reserved and personable. The lights went off at 9.00p.m. Sometimes, after the lights went off, he would come around and kiss us boys, like a father figure would. I didn't make anything of it. And then, one night, he came to my bed and *instead of kissing me good night,* **he took my hand and made me hold his penis in erection,** <u>over his</u> <u>cassock!!!</u> The whole thing might have last less than a minute. *I was very surprised!!!*

Then he went back to his room and I went to sleep…eventually.

Something very out of the ordinary had just happened to me,… My mother's words came back to my ears: *"priests can't do that!!! Priests don't do that!!!"*

The next day, not having anybody I could talk to about it, I kept thinking that *I had kind of held the penis of God!* They were teaching us to respect them as the representatives of God they were. And the last person I could have told that to …*was my own mother.* She used to tell us not to talk about priests even in good, by fear of saying something bad by accident! My mother, like the rest of *the bleating masses of the area,* had been brainwashed and conditioned to look at them and treat them like one treats God. I was sure that she would have taken the priest's side against me, *in spite of the fact that that priest had been caught in our own parish , playing with little boys, and sent away in another parish…which I found out 60 years later…* Somehow, in this instance, as a punishment, the stupid bishop had moved him *…in a seminary with over 350 young boys and young adults.* He must have looked at the gang of boys and rubbing his hands, licking his lips while watering at the mouth, must have said to himself: *"Yum! Yum! Dessert!!!"*

So I didn't say a word about it to anybody. But another priest came to me and asked me if something questionable had happened. Some other student in the infirmary had seen what had happened and had talked… I said yes and the next day or so, he asked me and one of my classmates, with whom I was friend, to do a job for him. He told us that we would go to the burning dump at about 600 feet behind the seminary, at the foot of the big mountain and there we were told to burn the contents of a large trunk.. The contents were the personal belongings and mementos of the priest who had *"molested"* me, as it is called nowadays.

And as to justify this action, he told us that that priest would not need his stuff anymore, since they were sending him to the asylum… (???) What that meant in 1951, was that he would be locked in the *"cuckoo's nest"*. That is the last I heard about that nurse priest. Did they really send him to a mental asylum??? Or did they move him to a new *"pasture"* of young flesh? I have my doubts. I'll tell you why.

Maybe 10 years ago, I have been told that, at the Vatican, there was a document instructing the bishops of the world how to deal with pedophile priests. The rule is like this. In the event that a priest would be found guilty of sexual abuse/pedophilia, to give money to the parents, to buy their silence and *to move that priest in another parish, far away.*

Remembering what happened to my sister who got punished for being a snitch, I never told my mother. She died over 30 years later without having found out. I was 13, in a dumbed down area, and something really out of the ordinary had just happen to me, and *I couldn't or wouldn't* tell anybody. Was I traumatized?

In a certain way, yes, I was. But I must throw some light on the subject. The traumatism was not of a sexual nature. I was from the farm, and one of our clandestine activities was masturbation in company of a sibling or a friend or alone. The problem was not of holding the penis of an adult. It was holding the penis of an adult "who never does these things because he's a priest, a man of God," and my mother taught us that "they don't do these things, even if you see them doing it to someone else or even to yourself." *Therefore, you are wrong and delusional in thinking he did that to you, end of story!!!*

If the law worked the same way for the leaders of the Catholic religion than for the laymen, I estimate there would be a couple of thousand bishops and cardinals…and at least 10-15 thousand priests in jail… A certain pope would also be in jail with them. All were actively involved in a conspiracy to cover up the sexual abuse by priests and not to report them to the judicial system. They were coerced by an edict of Pope John XXIII that was re-introduced and strengthened by an abdicating pope …in the last few years! In my books, they all deserve to be tried and sentenced to jail terms.

Could we see a whole slew of bishops in jail? I highly doubt it. When a religious or political leader commits an offense, suddenly, the law ceases to function… I'm not sure why! How many priests, bishops, cardinals, popes or prime ministers do we know who have ever been prosecuted and have paid for their crimes, like other criminals do???

"I reflected on other victims I had met and how they were raped right on the altars of their own churches. Some of them were altar boys, and they were abused before or after mass.

Charles L. Bailey Jr., *In the Shadow of the Cross*

Note to the reader and to you, Mario Jorge my brother.

Now, some might write comments on my web page and call me all kinds of names for choosing my path through life the way I see fit. Also for sharing my feelings about their choice of a path. I want you to know that I'm not doing it motivated by anger and a spirit of revenge against the Church and the priests. I really dislike priests for their sexual abuse of me (twice) when I was most vulnerable, of our children …and for their hypocrisy!

If I had wanted revenge, I could have sued the Catholic Church for compensation and punitive damages a long time ago. I didn't and I won't! SNAP(Survivors Network of those Abused by Priests) would have surely been able to advise me in that legal matter. I could have use them, for support and because I empathize with other victims of sex abuse by priests, but not for material gain. Why not? That's another question that some atheists and agnostics like me, might ask me in comments on my web page.

One of the reasons, Mario Jorge my brother,why I didn't sue these two priests, is because they themselves were the victims of a deranged religion forcing them to abstain from a normal sex life. They didn't have to stay or obey rules against nature, some might tell me. That is true.

But if you research the subject of intense indoctrination and sophisticated brainwashing from a young age, you'll realize that these priests were not "normal" human beings. They were brainwashed human beings and therefore were not intellectually and mentally free. They were somewhat like tele-guided robots. Prisoners in jail, deprived of a normal sex life, resort to sodomy even if they're not homosexuals… Mario Jorge my brother, that the Roman Curia likes it or not, we are sexual animals, and…sometimes, *just animals!*

End of the note.

The first thing I noticed, not long after you were elected pope, Mario Jorge my brother, you canonized two of your predecessors: John XXIII and John Paul II. To canonize a person, you must be absolutely sure that this person is in heaven and that he did at least two miracles recognized by the Church, as in this case, two cures.

So far, to my judgment, this is the first known mistake you committed. And I'm very nice in calling it a mistake... Maybe you got overwhelmed by the gigantic pressure that must surely have besieged you when you accepted the leadership of such a large and dubious organization. In canonizing John XXIII, you declared him a saint. Wikipedia define a saint as *"one who has been recognized for having an exceptional degree of holiness."* If we remember well, John XXIII wrote a certain edict about 70 years ago: *"The 69-page Latin document bearing the seal of Pope John XXIII was sent to every bishop in the world. The instructions outline a policy of 'strictest' secrecy in dealing with allegations of sexual abuse and threatens those who speak out with excommunication."*

World news The Observer

Is John XXIII's order to cover up crimes, in this case, what one would call *an exceptional degree of holiness?* Was that the work of God to order to hide from the law roughly 8-10 thousand priests guilty of children sexual abuse and over 2-3 thousand bishops who became accomplices after the fact?

Vatican releases figures on how it disciplined priests accused of sex abuse.

"UN committee against torture told that *848 priests have been defrocked* and *2572 given lesser sanctions in past decade."*

News. World news. Vatican.

It's a sad joke!!! This is about 10% of defrocked priests out of the total number of over 8-10 thousands abusers, in the last few years only. And only a few of them in jail! For those who would like to have a better idea of the scope of the worldwide epidemic, I recommend you check Wikipedia's document called:

Catholic Church sexual abuse cases.

That will give you an overview of the tragic situation threatening our children. I would conservatively assess that tragic situation at many million cases of abuses in the last 50 years alone. Sounds unbelievable? This astronomical number of millions of children sex abuse crimes, was made possible by the Vatican forcing bishops to let them continue, unpunished by the law! They were protected from the law that should have applied to them like it applies to any other criminals in advanced countries. And the Vatican is still not recognizing the criminal conduct of all the popes and the bishops since John XXIII, 70 years ago. *Mario Jorge my brother*, I hate to tell you that, by making John XXIII a saint, you have confirmed what I just said and *you have let down the youth of the world and 1.2 billion people(Catholics) looking up to you!*

There are thousands of victims of sexual abuse who do not care about the number of saints in heaven but who want justice, here on earth, –and in a foreseeable future– for the horrendous and mostly unpunished crimes against them!

Do the right thing; get justice for these children who are counting on you. Please, in their name, we are begging you!!! Let the United Nations apply the law to its fullest extent! Heads will fall where heads should! If you don't, you will have millions of crimes on your conscience. Millions of victims to whom you will have, with a clear and forewarned (...by me and others) mind, refused justice. And that, in order to cover up the people who have made those crimes possible by the cover up orders in the first place!

Finally, Mario Jorge my brother, if I say those things to you, it's because they have to be said, they have to be said loudly and to the right person! You are the right person; you have a good heart and the authority required to do it. The Roman Curia might not like it and might make some noise, *but ...not more than these millions of victims...*

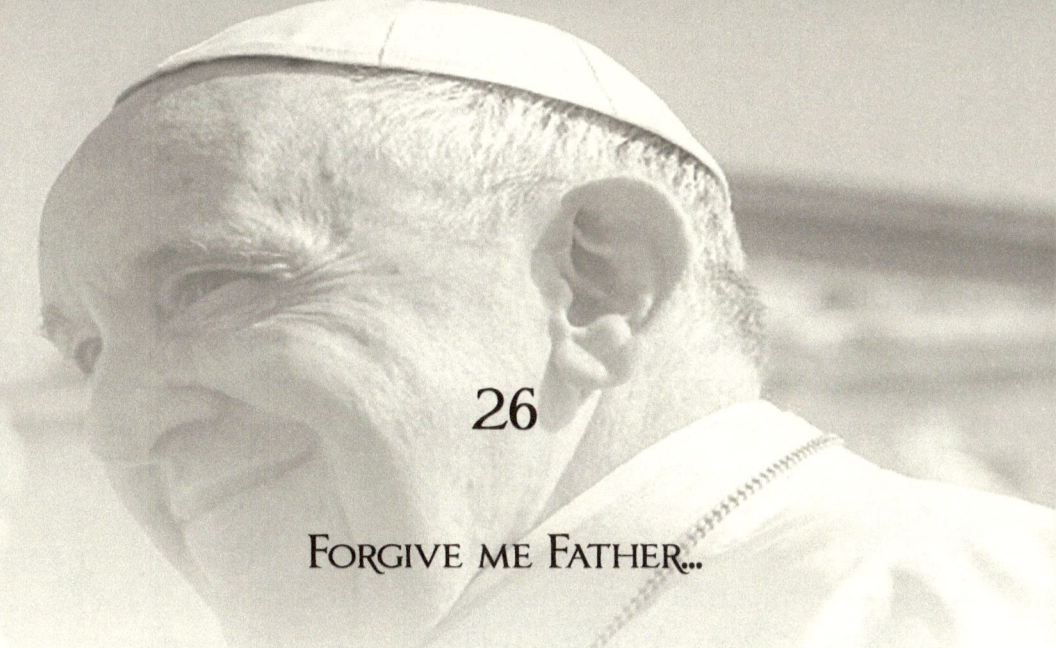

26

FORGIVE ME FATHER...

"I read a lot on the subject and had many conversations, and I have come to the conclusion that the Catholic Church is a force for evil."

Gabriel Byrne

I have been thinking long and hard to figure out what was the real motive behind the sacrament of confession. I finally accepted that they might believe that a man (a priest) could absolve most sins committed by man against another person or against God. It sounds pretty dumb to me, but we're talking about indoctrinated people here…

Mario Jorge my brother, here's my way of understanding religious confession and forgiveness by a third party. If you hit Mario on the head with a hammer, you go tell a priest; he makes a cross in the air and says: "Go in peace my son, your sin is forgiven." It doesn't do anything for Mario's concussion! But if you go and apologize to Mario and pay for a new hard hat (…for next time), you're digging in the right direction!

We got raised brainwashed into believing that if we said to somebody to eat shit, we had committed a venial sin. A venial sin was not a serious sin. But if you peeked at your sister's bum while she was climbing the

103

ladder you were holding, that was a mortal sin! And that, even if she had a chastity belt, metal panties and an armor like the one Joan of Arc wore!

Of course you could see nothing, but you had wished, you had hoped, you had desired to see maybe the shape or the contour of her genitals... So, having seen nothing should have cancelled the whole affair. But not in the Catholic Church!!! You had committed a mortal sin! And unless you went to confession and explicitly admit to the priest that you had tried to see your sister's bum, you were fried. You were guilty and deserving to go to hell for ever...on a one way ticket, *the same as the worst serial killer in the world.* And you might have been 10 years old! "Forever," when it's that hot, is a long time for a 10 year old who was only curious about his sister's anatomy ... *isn't it?*

You had no problem with me burning, in hell for eternity! But you have a problem with sending a priest to jail for a few well deserved years!!! And you're doing everything you can not to let that happen! And I don't believe for a second that it's for the sake of those priests! I believe it's to protect your cult's reputation so your Church doesn't lose face ... and paying customers (practicants)! To put it bluntly: to protect your own "derriere" and that of the members of the Roman Curia!

Really, Mario Jorge my brother, you know you are less good than God; would you throw a 10 year old nephew, who died so tragically in hell for eternity! for what he did or for anything a human being of any age would do? I didn't think you would or could! Do you consider God *as good as you are?* Why would He do to us what you, poor sinner, wouldn't be cruel enough to do? *What are you guys preaching, for God's sake???*

Mario Jorge my brother, you live among thousands of delusional men who have elevated themselves above the rest of humanity ...*and maybe above God himself!!!* The Vatican is probably the biggest Cuckoo's Nest of religious nuts in the world!!! *Run, Brother, RUN, while you can!!!*

P.S.

Would you please say Hi! to Jack for me? (…Jack Nicholson, Yeah!)

Just kidding, Brother…

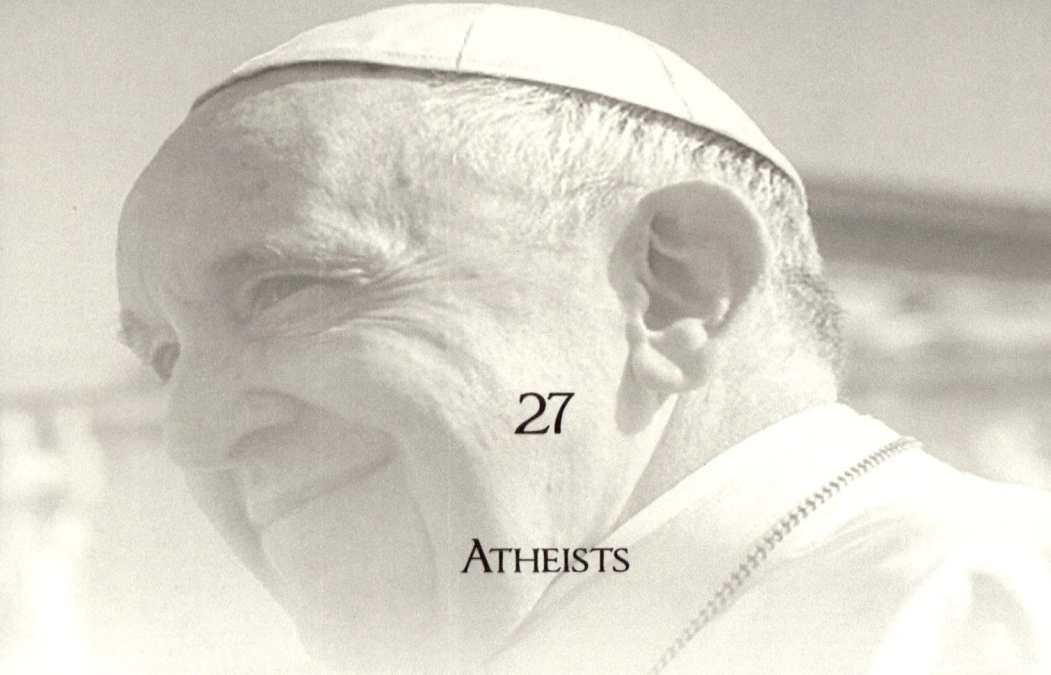

27

ATHEISTS

"Shake off all the fears of servile prejudices, under which weak minds are servilely crouched. Fix reason firmly in her seat, and call on her tribunal for every fact, every opinion. Question with boldness even the existence of a God; because, if there be one, he must more approve of the homage of reason than that of blindfolded fear."

Thomas Jefferson (1743 1826)

When I was young, the word atheist had one of the most pejorative connotations of the French language. There was nothing dirtier and lower that one could accuse someone of being. In our view, one had to be very bad and crazy for daring to question the teachings of the Catholic Church, and doubt the existence of God.

I no longer have that biased opinion that was poisoning my mind. I was judging and condemning them, despite the fact that religion was teaching us to love our enemies. "But not atheists!" We had the right and were encouraged to hate them. Who did they think they were, to share infaillibility?

106

Mario Jorge my brother, the winds have shifted. The Catholic Church might just have lost face, it seems. How will it get out of the precarious position where it put itself in during the last few decades and particularly, in the last ten years? It has no chance of getting out of that precarious position without losing a lot of feathers. Although the big guys protect each other, it will very likely end up with serious bruises to its reputation and be seen for what it really is: a very questionable organization. There are lots of skeletons in the Vatican's closets... And without being specific, some of them are even more serious than the scandal of our children it has sexually abused and the infamous cover-up of those crimes.

I'm not an atheist, but I would not be ashamed of it , if I was. Between what they believe and what I believe, there is less distance than between what the Catholic Church preaches and what I believe. In fact, I believe absolutely nothing of what the Catholic Church preaches, except for the advice: *"Do unto others as you would like them do unto you."* As we have seen before, this command already existed 600 years before the coming of Jesus. It's therefore not a Catholic Church original finding!

You might be surprised by my conception of an atheist. For me, Mario Jorge my brother, an atheist is typically a self-respecting person who respects the intelligence and human reason in man, who does not deny himself/herself to soothe his/her fear of the unknown, including the afterlife. This person has the courage to live without the promise that there is an afterlife. This person is braver than most Catholic people! One might conclude that atheists are careless and are not aware of the serious risks inherent to their spiritual orientation. Research has shown that the opposite seems to be true...

If I was put in the situation of having a roommate and that roommate would be either a bishop or an atheist, I would have no hesitation about whom to cohabit with... *especially if she was personable and didn't dress like a drag queen!* Life is short, Brother, you should laugh while you're still kicking… And don't take yourself too seriously; nobody else does… I mean… take *themselves* too seriously. Ha Ha!

28

SYSTEMATIC DENIGRATION OF WOMEN

"This notion that women are somehow inferior to men is not restricted to one religion, one belief. Women are restricted to play a full and equal role in many faiths. Nor that, tragically, the influence of this design stops at the walls of the church, mosque, synagogue, or temple. This indiscriminating attitude unjustifiably attributed to the supreme authority, has provided a reason or excuse for the lack of equal rights of women, worldwide, for centuries. And at its most disgusting level, the belief that women must be subjugated to the whims of men serves as an excuse for slavery, violence, forced prostitution, genital mutilation and national laws excluding rape from the ranks of crime.

But ... it also deprives millions of girls and women from the control over their own bodies and their lives, and it continues to deny them access to education, health, employment and influence within their own community ... The truth is that male religious leaders have had-and still have-an option to interpret the scriptures, either to exalt or subjugate women, for their own selfish purposes, and they chose overwhelmingly to subjugate them" Jimmy Carter (former President of the United States) *Losing My Religion for Equality.*

Mario Jorge my brother, it seems that Christian religions have done more than their share to denigrate women. If a company or an individual in America, today, would do half as much against women, they would be severely punished by law.

One of the problems in the world is the relentlessness that man has used against women. The Bible, whose religious and spiritual value I question seriously, abounds with degrading comments towards women: *"No wickedness comes anywhere near the wickedness of a woman......Sin began with a woman and thanks to her we all must die"* (Ecclesiasticus 25:19,24).

Jewish Rabbis listed nine curses inflicted on women as a result of the Fall: *"To the woman He gave nine curses and death: the burden of the blood of menstruation and the blood of virginity; the burden of pregnancy; the burden of childbirth; the burden of bringing up the children; her head is covered as one in mourning; she pierces her ear like a permanent slave or slave girl who serves her master; she is not to be believed as a witness; and after everything--death."*

To the present day, orthodox Jewish men, in their daily morning prayer, recite: *"Blessed be God King of the universe that Thou has not made me a woman."* Saint Augustine, Bishop of Hippo Regius (354 – 430) said: *"What a difference whether it's a wife or mother? We must always look out for that temptress Eve who remains in every woman? I fail to see what use can man make of the woman, if one excludes the function of raising children."*

And the misogynist Catholic Church chose to give him as an example to the world by making him a saint!!! Centuries later, St. Thomas Aquinas still considered Women as defective: *"As for her individual nature, woman is defective and poorly raised, since the active force contained in the male seed (semen) tends to produce a perfect likeness of the masculine sex. On the other hand the production of a woman comes from a defect in the active force or from a lack of a certain matter or even from an external influence.*" And the Catholic Church also made him a saint!!!

Finally, Martin Luther could not see any benefit from a woman other than to bring in the world as many children as possible, regardless of the residual effects: *"If they become tired or die, it has no importance. Let them die in childbirth, that's why they are there." "Again and again all women are denigrated because of the image of Eve the temptress, thanks to the Genesis account."*

Comments on Bible sexism by Syed Yusuf

When I was young, in Québec, women had to confess for having had an orgasm... They should not participate in the sexual act; they should be the submissive recipient, aiming for a possible offspring, *period!!!* Or be a tool to enable the poor man to dump his seminal fluid *surplus when it suited him...*

"Man is neither angel nor beast. But the problem is that, who wants to act as an angel ends up acting as a beast!" (Author's translation from French.)"

Pascal

I do not know if it's just me, but if I had been a woman, in the last 50 years, I would have given a piece of my mind to the Catholic Church *and its irrational cult it calls...a religion.* I do not think it was a human and intelligent way to treat women and, by extension, man who was encouraged to disrespect his life partner, his best friend, the mother of his children and *to only use her as a contraption for his seminal fluid surplus dumpsite and a **domestic slave!***

It's unfortunate that they have considered my mother as if she was less than a mother rabbit. My mother was more than a uterus serving the perverse agenda of the Church and of the State, which more often than not, share the same bed ...political bed that is.

Religion was putting people to sleep, and trained them never to speak up in church or in the parliament and tell the priest or the Prime Minister their objections. Some might have considered interrupting one of those power hungry psychopaths, but it was the equivalent of a social suicide. It would have meant rejection from the whole village, and ending up a pariah and certain to be excommunicated ...if not anathematized!

The denigration of women by men began long before the organized ...*and organizing religions.* I think that man has always tended to belittle women. Physically stronger, in general, he could force any and all women to a subordinate role. I believe that man had and perhaps still has, in some cases, an inferiority complex towards women.

"Mario Jorge my brother, I can only see one explanation of the phenomenon: man always saw the woman as a superior being that he envies because she can co-create human beings and he can't! To maintain his supposed superiority in front of the other males, he resorted to psychological and physical subjugation and even bullying, if and when necessary."

If we agree on the fact that the mother has a key role within the family, we must also consider all other complementary factors that are critical in the structure of the whole family. The father, which, I hope, I have not pulled down a peg too many, has a different role than that of the mother, but an equally important role. As with the mother, his role is multiple.

He must first demonstrate toward his wife a total commitment to this mission they have chosen–*or accepted*– in some cases, and a team spirit on which she can rely on at all time, 24/7. He should try, if there are other children than the newborn, to promote a peaceful ambience and an atmosphere propitious to the comfort and smooth running of the family, especially during the first months.

The more the baby will grow, the more the life of the mother will regain some normalcy. The interaction with other children, if it's the case, should be guided and encouraged whenever possible. This is the first phase of belonging and connecting that the baby will experience, and it is of the utmost importance.

"You are 100% responsible for how your children turn out. And you accomplish that by teaching them they are 100% responsible for how they turn out."

Peter Keostenbau

Finally, I believe that if in 2023 we find ourselves in the unstable situation that we observe around the world, it's because we have divided humanity into two entities. First there is the world of men with their phallocratic way to subjugate women and keep them away from worldly affairs. And then there is the world of women and children. And until women are respected for what and who they are and treated at least as equal, humanity will continue its erratic and cruel journey leading to self-destruction. We are more technologically advanced than the Cro-Magnons, but no more civilized and probably less.

"It's called civilization. Women invented it, and every time you men blow it all to bits, we just invent it again."

Orson Scott Card, The Folk of the Fringe

29
THE ESSENCE OF A WOMAN

"To call woman the weaker sex is a libel; it is man's injustice to woman. If by strength is meant brute strength, then, indeed, is woman less brute than man. If by strength is meant moral power, then woman is immeasurably man's superior."

Mahatma Gandhi (*To the Women of India (Young India,* Oct. 4, 1930)

B y her ability to procreate, she was created with internal and external organs necessary for the gestation of children and their survival. All her female biological design allows her to complete the reproduction of a human being in less than 40 weeks... I wish I could do that! But God looked at me and thought: " *Nah! Men are not smart enough to be co-creator with me!* For me, it is without a doubt, the greatest miracle of the whole creation.

Men might retort to me that women don't do that alone. They need men! Yes, they do! Fertilization of the ovum is certainly required for that mystery to happen, but it is much less complex than gestation. However, in spite of its capital role in the whole operation, it takes *at least 3 minutes* of our busy schedule ...on a good day...

"Mario Jorge my brother, I'm not sure that how the spermatozoid will win the race against other spermatozoids – without asking for directions...– and

help change the egg into a zygote, makes any difference in the development of the foetus... Our job, us males, is to deliver at the right moment... and all moments are right for us... We do not mind having to make deliveries every day —or night— for that matter, if necessary... We are very generous in that department!!!"

The spermatozoid and egg have met; the spermatozoid has moved in, and the conception has begun. The woman has just entered a process that will change her complete hormonal system, which, in turn will trigger a chain reaction throughout her whole body, both physiological and psychological. For the sake of the case, she will become a factory of millions of individual cells producing different components with different functions. We create human tissue in the lab today, but we will never create a *genuine* human being without using an egg and a spermatozoid. God has the copyright on the human being design! *"Human gestation is the most beautiful phenomenon in the whole of creation."*

A computer is a mechanical machine but mainly electronic, very complicated that very few people know how to manufacture, and that even fewer can understand. It is a magical gadget, if you want, but just a gadget that can't do anything that it has not been previously programmed to do, by a Homo sapiens.

As the futurist Alvin Toffler was already *saying* in *Future Shock*, circa 1970, one day we will build a robot, with a striking human appearance, which will be difficult to differentiate from a human being. It will speak with the appropriate facial expressions. It's incredible! But believe me it will never experience the feelings and emotions that are our lot. A one day old child has an incredibly larger potential than any contraption we will ever concoct!

Woman, therefore, this creation agent, can produce a human being whose brain alone exceeds in capacity and creativity all present and future computers, many times over. And we only use about 10% of the capacity of our brains, according to some experts. Some might tell me, that the woman has nothing to do with the complexity and power of the human brain that takes shape in her womb for nine long months. It is very possible; I don't know. Maybe the embryo grows like a plant in the garden...

But Mario Jorge my brother, is it possible that from the 90% of the brain that we don't use most of the time, the woman uses it to a certain degree higher than man does? If we believe in a creator or a creative force that causes everything to exist, is it possible that the brain works at 99% of its capacity in certain circumstances of life, and that reproduction and nurturing are some of them? The experts will probably not agree and say that it's not possible, but these are probably men in a situation we call a conflict of interest...

It would be interesting for a moment to consider this assumption, if I may. Let's accept, as a premise of this hypothesis, that it is false that the brain operates at only 10% of its capacity. If we have a brain that is 10 times more powerful than what we can use or seem to need, then how to explain the superfluous and useless 90% portion of it? How to explain that waste, since science tells us that nothing is created and nothing is lost in the creation. I find it hard to believe that it is by accident that we would have 10 times more "brains" than we need!

God could have created one sex and that creature could have been hermaphrodite like we find in a few species in the animal kingdom. But for some reason, Mario Jorge my brother, He thought that it would be more fun if He complicated the game and told man:

"This woman is a people manufacturer. If you want an heir, you have to try and connect with her and hope that she shows some cooperation toward a relation and a collaboration conducive to an union of the reproduction contraption towards copulation starting a gestation ending in the procreation of a unit of population augmentation at time of completion..."

"For women, the best aphrodisiacs are words. The Gspot is in the ears. He who looks for it below there is wasting his time."

Isabel Allende, Of Love and Shadows

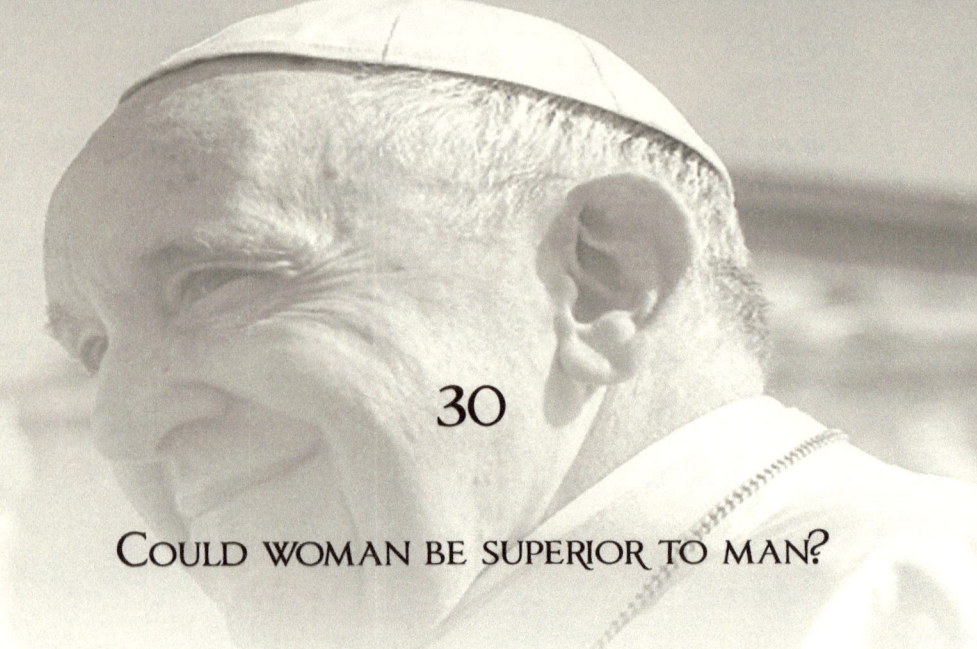

30

Could woman be superior to man?

"The woman contains the social problem and the human mystery. She seems the great weakness, she is the great strength." (Author's translation from French.)

Victor Hugo

Mario Jorge my brother, you would never believe what happens next. I just got back from lunch and chatting with my wife Judy about my thesis on the natural superiority of women. She looked at me with the air of saying: "Are you blind?" And without missing a beat she added: "Where were you for the last 50 years? Hast thou not heard about *The Natural Superiority of Women*, by Ashley Montagu??? Everyone knows that women are superior!!!" And noting my surprise, she must have added in her heart of hearts: "Hast thou ever looked at me? Do you know who you're talking to, *you miserable breeder of the male species?"Ha!Ha!*

I remembered that we, of the male species, are stronger and …I tiptoed back to my computer room, my tail between my legs, while she was still in a relatively good mood…Ha! Ha! So I'm not the only one thinking that women are superior. And I must say that, honestly, I had never heard of another weirdo advancing such a thesis. I promise you one thing: that's a book that I will buy and read with a lot of excitement.

Without delay, I ordered and received the book, *The Natural Superiority of Women*. I already read it ...*twice*. I find it very, very interesting, in spite of the fact that it's heavy reading. Dr. Ashley Montagu graduated in psychology and in anthropology, he taught anatomy in 5 prestigious American universities. He was a professor of anthropology, a social biologist, and I don't know what else. He demonstrated the biological superiority of women based on his knowledge but also on the work of many other researchers. His researches have convinced me that I had good reasons to believe that the woman is naturally superior, without really knowing why. I could still change my text, and use his arguments, but I prefer to remain original and not hide behind the knowledge of others, at the risk of being wrong.

Once we accept that women are biologically and mentally superior to men –if we accept it at all– we should ask ourselves what it implies.

"I gladly would agree that women are superior to us, if it could deter them from pretending they're our equals."(Author's translation from French)

Sacha Guitry

Following his attitude, you can take it two ways. The first one, we can sit, look her up and tell ourselves: "This Cro-Magnon, somehow, is more powerful than me. She threatens my reputation and my supposed superiority in front of other men ...and of other women. I cannot let that happen. I'll show her who's the boss! She has no choice; I'm stronger than her. There is no question that she hunts, goes to war or to work other than as a servant or a subordinate. *After all, she's only a woman!* And especially she would be better not to put her nose, in man's business, like the public affairs! Her job at best, is to take care of me and of the kids I so generously gave her and honored her with!"

With this first attitude towards women, we find ourselves in 2023, in our Tower of Babel, with wars and threats of atomic war or worse, biological warfare, the political and economic disarray at the global level, hunger, crimes, murders, terrorism, global warming and the list continues.

"The oppression of a people or even a single individual is the oppression of all and no one can violate freedom of one without violating the freedom of everyone."

Mikhail Bakunin

The second attitude, Mario Jorge my brother is, for me, the most promising and the most creative of a humane future which should not lead to the Tower of Babel. You might be wondering how I imply that the way we treat women in the world, the reduced role that some countries allow them to play, can have a possible connection with the serious problems we are facing globally. Remember: *"…no one can violate freedom of one without violating the freedom of everyone."*

I maintain that the woman is superior to man by her vocation, her mission, and her nurturing nature. She shapes the body of her child, and I think she knows how to shape the mind and the heart of a human being, a genuine human being, which may become a self-actualized "Homo sapiens!"

"Women are better able to establish the pedagogy of the future and to guarantee to tomorrow's students an adequate education to handle the challenges ahead."

Marc Gendron

I believe that this power I was talking about applies to both men and women, but more so to women. It may not be that women have a power rated 12, by comparison to men, who have a power rated 10. I would rather see it like this. Since I love mechanics, I will draw an example from mechanics. Suppose you have an electric car that works with batteries that you recharge overnight, like your cell phone. And let's say your husband has exactly the same car.

If you weigh 125 lbs and he weighs 125 lbs, on the same trajectory, you should get the same range on a battery charge. But if he weighs 250 lbs, he cannot travel the same distance than you do, the cargo being double. Her tool is perfectly identical to yours and so is the path. She accomplishes more than you, she produces more than you, if we talk distance; but her tool is not more powerful than yours, and she doesn't drive better than you do.

What she has less of, the weight, allows her to win the race in terms of distance or range. Could it be that what gives a natural superiority to women, is something that men have and that it represents a handicap that women might not have? And since women had kind of been put on a shelf for, let say 15 thousand years, at least, is it possible that they were somehow spared from the dehumanization caused and experienced by men who were the authors and the victims of that dehumanization?

Is it possible, Mario Jorge my brother, that man, the hunter, the warrior and *the tyrant towards others*, especially towards women, would somehow still be traumatized at the archetypes level? And is it possible that *his* greed, *his* lust for power, *his* obsession with power, *his* abuse of power, the corrupted politics of *his* governments, *his* unjust justice system, *HIS* religions, the abuse of humans, mostly perpetrated by *him*, is it possible that all those monstrosities could have ended up, in some ways, affecting man negatively?

Modern man is very different from the Cro-Magnon. Different in the sense of being more advanced and technologically better equipped. But could he somehow have partially degenerated? We sometimes say when speaking about a person that he/she is a human wreck. We hear about soldiers returning from combat with a serious problem called "post-traumatic stress disorder." We hear more and more about it. Could man suffer from a kind of post-traumatic stress disorder following his barbarian conduct of the last 15,000 years or maybe of the last 15 million years? I'll ask a more direct and simple question. Why is man of the 20th and of the 21st century as destructive and stupid, as cruel and barbaric? Why the wars, the terrorism, the oppression of peoples, the murders, the sexual slavery, the genital mutilations, and the almost universal denigration of women?

We (men) will have to correct our conduct and ...ask women for forgiveness!

Frankly, Mario Jorge my brother, I am ashamed to belong to the human race, especially being a male and being a part of the gender of the animal the most stupid, the most cruel, the most vicious of all this beautiful creation! I want right here and now, on behalf of the people of the earth, sincerely apologize to women of the world who have been victims of men's perpetual inferiority complex and macho attitude, which, I believe, push man to enslave and humiliate women. how us, men, could, not only do it, but do it for 15 thousand or 15 million years and justify our conduct as if it were correct and then ...to dare think that we are superior to women???

When we commit such crimes against women and against humanity in general, one day it catches up with us and we shall amend! And that day has arrived, it is now! And the worst part is that women, who had nothing to do with it, have paid- and _will continue_- to pay for it too. _That is not fair! Could the creator have fallen asleep in Her rocking chair? Or ... could He be a man?_

Tell me, Mario Jorge my brother, will men reading this advocacy, make a literary analysis of it without worrying about the anthropological value of my honest and sincere intervention to the defense of justice for women, even if it is belated? Will they let this emergency call to all of mankind, go down in their heart to finally put an end to this tragic and senseless cold war between men **and the woman?**

"Never underestimate the power of human stupidity.

Robert Heinlein

I have questioned myself during my life about this shameful situation and I asked myself even more intensely in the recent months, and at the risk of sounding like an idiot or a traitor, I have no doubt as to the conclusion of this argument. I cannot deny that, for me, the natural superiority of women is not a fable; *it is a fact!*

Many men will not like my conclusion! *It's too bad...*

31

TRIBUTE TO ALL MOTHERS IN THE WORLD

"The loving mother teaches her child to walk alone."

Sören Kierkegaard

*M*ario Jorge my brother, of all the professions, the vocations, of all the roles humans can assume, the vocation of mother is unparalleled! We, men, can be prime minister of a country, king, or pope, **but only a woman can be a mother**. The closest one can be to the creator is to be co-creator.

A woman, by her nature and her vocation, if she chooses to, will lend her body and her whole being for the realization in her, of the greatest mystery in the universe. She —and she alone— can fulfill this function that sublimates her. The relationship of a child to his mother is probably the image of our relationship to our Supreme Being. Left to themselves, women don't need any lessons, nor university training to fulfill this miraculous task.

*They were created with this procreation option, and all the necessary mechanisms to achieve this mysterious and sacred operation. And **only** if they choose to participate in this mystery, **if they wish**, they can allow a world of wonders to develop within themselves. If you can read this, thank* *a teacher, but more importantly, thank your mother! She accomplished the greatest and the most noble act of generosity and selflessness that can be asked from a human being.*

The greatest of privileges and the greatest of honors have been vested in them and for all the sacrifices and the deprivations that the fulfillment of this mystery implies, they deserve our admiration, our sincere gratitude and respect.

My sincere love and deepest respect to all of you, WOMEN!!!

A WOMAN!

Mysterious creature, the symbol of beauty,

In the whole creation, there is nothing better.

The pinnacle of art, faithful to your duty,

You cause my heart to race, and my eyes to flutter.

We call you flirtatious, and of man seductive,

We call you saint or wise or even mad woman,

We even crown you Queen, of the human beehive,

But my preferred title: you are a jewel for man.

You are the measure of all that is beautiful,

The dominant of all art museums display,

Leonardo da Vinci, painted you quite playful,

And most of the artists prefer you, to this day.

Of all God's master pieces, you are the pinnacle,

Made you co-creator, mother of God made thee.

You are smart and witty, oh! What a spectacle,

To notice your wisdom, accurate to a tee.

Man always envied you he is scared and jealous,

Of your superiority in so many aspects,

But the worse of them all, man, with all due respect,

Cannot give birth to kids, and that drives him callous.

Not able to compete, he could cooperate.

But instead to join her, he chose to bully her

Using subjugation, and thus at a great rate,

Forced her to compliance, and usurped her power.

Stronger physically, but obsessed by his greed,

His insecurity; unable to compete,

With this beautiful soul, should have chosen to heed

But instead turned bossy, and her mission impede.

Creation without you would be absurdity.

Your nurturing talent, and the size of your heart,

Gone from the creation, would be an oddity,

That we cannot afford Oh! Believe me Sweetheart.

Reclaim your right to be the backbone of the world,

We need your moral strength and your resourcefulness,

To bring back to this earth, the most beautiful word,

This feeling we call love, Please in all its fullness.

Composed this July 1, 2014.

Roméo Gauvreau

CONCLUSION

What we expect and ask you to do, Mario Jorge my brother, will not go quietly. The Catholic Church needs a very invasive surgery that threatens its survival. Any surgery should be avoided when there are alternatives medecines offering as much chances of success but a lot less risks. This is a situation that we, as individuals, already had to face or will possibly face in our own lifetime. In the case of the Catholic Church, I see no gentle methods that could solve problems of such a large scale as the children sexual abuse by priests and the subjugation/denigration of women.

First there is the sexual abuse itself which is a crime punishable by law and, hopefully, a jail sentence. Then there is the policy of the Vatican ordering the bishops of the world to cover up these crimes and their perpetrators and buy the silence of parents and of victims / children with money. As we have seen, the UN is currently investigating and has intimated the Vatican to cooperate with the local laws of each jurisdiction. How the Vatican will deal with such a challenge/deadlock remains to be seen.

Second, there's the denigration of women through the scriptures which reinforce the phallocratic and macho attitude of men towards women, including "men of the cloth" ...and their celibacy!

As the pope, Mario Jorge my brother, you're on the hot seat! You're facing a serious dilemma. You know the inhumane Vatican's policy on sexual abuse. You know that following the ultimatum of the United Nations, the Vatican no longer has the option to maintain the "status quo"

There are also two other very important problems to solve: the celibacy of priests and the ordination of women! The responsibility is yours; you are the Pope and the King of Vatican city. Will you dare throw the ball in the direction of the solution to the serious problems of the Catholic Church? And doing so, possibly alienate a large majority of cardinals and bishops who are part of the government of the Church in the strict sense? What are you going to do?

Good success to you and we will continue having your back. We're pulling with you! If it can be done, *You can do it!* Dear Mario Jorge, I love you like the brother I feel you are to all of us...*and we will stay tuned!*

"Nothing can do what a book can do. Lifts you out of your life... to a whole new world, whole new perspective. A book is like a dream you're borrowing from a friend."

Dave Kellett,

Say brothers, say sisters,

I love you, all of you.

Roméo

Dec 24 2023